Issues: New magazine design

Issues: New magazine design

Written and designed by Jeremy Leslie

Published in 2000 by Laurence King Publishing
an imprint of Calmann & King Ltd
71 Great Russell Street
London WC1B 3BN
Tel: +44 20 7831 6351
Fax: +44 20 7831 8356
e-mail: enquiries@calmann-king.co.uk
www.laurence-king.com

A catalogue record for this book is available from
the British Library.

ISBN 1 85669 177 2

Printed in Hong Kong

Contents

'The magazine is not one kind of thing, but many – it is defined by its repetitive publication and little else. Certainly not by its content, and increasingly not by its form.'

I don't read magazines. And neither, I suspect, do you. But I enjoy them, I celebrate them, I am even perhaps mentally addicted to them, to judge by the piles in my home and workplace. But read them? That would be a curious way to set about their pleasures.

All this is to say that magazines – at least ones that really celebrate the medium – are for looking at as much as they are for reading. We need a new word for what we do when we experience them.

Magazines are the dangerous friends of books, always twitching to subvert a rule or two. At the same, time they are the smart relations of newspapers, so much better dressed in paper, ink and binding. Whether about world affairs, a curious hobby, fashion or some area even more ephemeral, they tend to set the aspiration, pitch standards, and go beyond the throwaway event of newsprint or the instant history of a broadcast to give us the illusion of substance. Even a salacious people-watching magazine has the aura of an 'organ-of-record' in a way that smeary newsprint struggles to achieve.

Besides floating clear of their print cousins, and holding on to time in a way that eludes the remorselessly linear experience of television, magazines are even the vibrant precursors and inspiration for websites (more on that later). When we pick up a magazine we do not read, or have to read. We look and we interact. Magazines had the rudiments of hypertext (multiple links between content) before the concept was even dreamt up in the 1960s, let alone the world wide web made browse-able in the 1990s. Magazines invite us to browse, to graze, to choose the direction we jump in. We sample an eyeful of imagery here and a mouthful of words there, and continue with no intention other than being 'infotained'. Reading – if we ever do finally read a text from beginning to end – comes only

at the end of a process of sifting and sampling.

The balance between seeking entertainment and finding information varies according to our wants or needs, and according to the selected magazine, but there is nearly always, even in the driest of publications, some pleasuring of the reader. The delivery of information takes a path that is somewhere between clarity and succinctness, or is discursively stimulating at the expense of predictability and transparency. Usually, almost inevitably, a magazine combines elements of both routes. In this the magazine veers between the rational and the intuitive, seeking response from both sides of the brain.

Jeremy Leslie's analysis of magazine form and recent experimentations demonstrates just how vibrant the present industry is in creative terms. But what underlies that activity? In search of answers, we can benefit from revisiting the origin of the medium.

Magazines emerged in England at the beginning of the eighteenth century: initially, they were a weekly, more analytical and polemical variant of the newspaper, which was still close to its newsletter origins of a century previous. In two journals, *The Tatler* and *The Spectator* (both still with us, and even with complementary web forms, although the former has transmogrified into something with little connection to its origin), the medium quickly reached significance, giving space to essayists who helped drive the political and cultural agenda. American and continental magazines were swift to follow, although various laws relating to publications and taxes often threatened the basic economic model, along with limits on distribution.

As with any developing industry, magazine publishers always tested the form, pushing it into new areas – driven mostly by the pressures for economy of means set against the fickle needs of their readers always seeking fresh attractions. The

early magazine often plagiarized content from books and other magazines, taking advantage of non-existent copyright legislation in the same way that still applies, for example, in some eastern European and Far East countries. But the profit-motive was by no means the only driving imperative: magazine history is also littered with innovation driven by propagandist ends.

Consider for example, *The Penny Magazine*, published from 1832. This was a pioneer in the extensive use of woodcut illustration, but was not driven to innovate in a quest for readers' money. It set a low price, and took an expensive production option. It was published in England by the Society for the Diffusion of Useful Knowledge and was devised to draw the interest of the educated artisan. The rapid advances in the illustrated magazine during the mid to late nineteenth century continued to combine this quest for the mind and pocket of the increasingly educated masses with an appropriation of developing technologies, bringing illustration styles into life, partly driven by the potential of the plates and the presses.

A key factor, often ignored, in the development of the structure and design of magazines (and a dominant factor today) was the growth of advertising in the later nineteenth century. This jumped rapidly from being a source of extra revenue to becoming a key component in the economic model. Publishers realized that they needed to set the price according to the pocket of the target reader if they wanted to maximize their competitiveness for attracting readers and advertisers; and that if they then delivered a suitably large market they could charge advertisers a higher rate that would subsidize the print costs and deliver the profit. Magazine publishing became for the most part in capitalist economies a business based on building communities of readers that could be sold to as

Foreword
by Lewis Blackwell

well as informed and entertained. Increasingly, the focus of the advertising base drove the form of many publications. As the sophistication of marketing techniques grew in the second half of the twentieth century, so advertisers became more demanding about how ads worked in magazines, leading to the ads and the agencies that created and booked them having a major role in the shaping of the look and feel of magazines - even if inadvertently, in that art directors would have to design their magazines to offset the impact of the ads around the editorial. This factor has a lot to say for the experience of content order and its weighting in many publications.

Only those magazines that have a relatively high cover price or low production values, or have no need to succumb to the profit motive, can fight the effect of ads, which can be like a random virus spread across the publisher's orderly pages. And what kind of magazines don't follow profits? Unprofitable ones. Which either fail, or else are supported for the purposes of propaganda. Whether a political manifesto, a charity's call for alms, a company's in-house quarterly, or a parish newsletter, propaganda has to be the thing that drives the operation when ads don't.

The issue of how the item is funded, and therefore how much it costs the reader and how much 'value' is represented in the messaging, invites us into the discussion of just what a magazine is. When is it not a book? Or a newspaper? When is it art? From early in magazine history, there have been magazines that have tested the description, produced with resources that in some way broke the common model, or in other form-busting ways that tested the boundaries of our understanding of the medium. Contrast an art magazine such as *Jugend*, which achieved popularity in Vienna at the beginning of the twentieth century at the same time as pushing an artistic movement (Jugendstil), with *De Stijl*, which also spurred a movement in Holland from 1917 while being mainly subsidized by editor/designer Theo van Doesburg. Was one more a magazine than the other? Was the latter a series of artworks? The rest of this century has seen numerous other innovations, whether for propagandist or for profitable motives, that questioned the magazine form to the point of destruction, or at least deconstruction.

So to the present, heading into the eye of the future. Here we are, beset by media theory

and wild excitement about the internet undermining all previous mass-media at the same time as serious doubt at whether the web can replace, rather than augment.

On past performance of new mass-media appearing, the magazine should be safe. Film, radio and television have not killed each other off, nor have they held back print. All have flourished, to the point that there are more magazines now than there were ten years ago, more radio and television stations after the arrival of internet than before. But endless growth would seem unlikely, given limited physical resources and a likely rise in the cost of the key raw material of paper as environmental pressures grow.

A key issue in the development of new media is suggested by the explosion of mass-media: that somebody out there must be watching it. Lots of it. How and why they are doing that across other mass-communication affects the development of the magazine.

Research in 1999 on the habits of American youth suggested that they consumed a staggering 40 hours of media per week (the same time as the traditional working week!), split between television, computer games, videos, audio systems and the internet. Given the demands of all that time, it is no surprise to find that they were not reading much … compared to eight hours a day on the electronic media, they were spending half an hour a day reading print. Trusting that those 30 minutes were not taken up by deciphering a CD booklet, or that the only magazine they read was the US bestseller *TV Guide*, it is daunting to question how magazines (let alone books) find a slot in a teenager's infotainment schedule.

The reaction may already have come in the intensity, and more intuitive 'reads' of youth magazines where the type and image are rich melds of information that go beyond the look of screen media … the *Raygun* genre of graphic design. This has now largely passed, and indeed that magazine has suffered, from its failure to do what print does spectacularly well – deliver a reading experience. Perhaps this is why the 'deconstructed' or 'grunge' aesthetic in some magazine design has been replaced by a ferociously cool typographic aesthetic that apes late 1950s and early 1960s modernism – a territory that is also beyond the capacity of web designers for the most part today, through preference and

through tools. A fine example of this switch was apparent in the direction taken by the art director and publisher Terry Jones with his magazine *i-D*; after years of graphic expressionism, in 1997 the magazine moved back to a rigour and clarity that made it once again stand out from its peer group, and also made it a source of longer text and highly considered still imagery – something not available from the screen.

A combination of marketing's soft science, and the new imperatives of e-commerce, means that the modern webzine is the product of very different pressures to those which built the look and feel of the print magazine over many years. Webzines are going from infancy to great sophistication within a decade. Just as for print, there are studies tracking how the reader's eye falls from image to caption to headline to, just maybe, the main text (but not necessarily at the beginning), so there are 'useability' tests on websites that show how viewers relate in very different ways to online magazines. The crudeness of behavioural measurement in these models are driving the similarities of many major early sites.

But at the same time as this path is taken by many major business ventures, the web offers virtually free publication possibilities for lesser operations. An internet service provider account, a few megabytes of server space, some enthusiasm and a little HTML knowledge is all you need to make some kind of webzine. The results are beyond counting: it would be hard to discount that much of the experimental energy that used to go into print, does not now in part go into such sites. In contrast to print magazines, the cost of making and the access to distribution is much less of an issue.

As to the future of the electronic magazine, we have to jump beyond the computer screen and consider how the emerging integration of the web and the mobile phone offers the most likely route for webzines. There we have a developing medium that combines the portability and convenience of the magazine with the interactivity and updating potential of the web. While the current low-res mono screen of a phone hardly equates to a colour A4 page, it has other strengths. This is not an 'if' but a definite, and how we export magazine factors to that environment will be intriguing to explore in time.

But back to print, the glorious tactile field of most of our subjects. There are studies that show

how magazine content has shifted dramatically over recent years – in the past decade it has been estimated that image content has increased eight-fold, a result of the liberation of page content by digital technology and by the increasing cheapness of colour print, along with the pressure to maintain allure in the context of image-rich rival media. Some research suggests that magazine circulations are in decline; other research says there has never been more. Both are probably right - because the magazine is moving from mass-communication to increasingly targeted messaging. This is in reaction to the likes of those American teenagers and others being increasingly non-social individuals; as Western society features people pursuing their own path for infotainment, so magazines reflect this and serve new, somewhat solipsistic needs.

As said above, the magazine is not one kind of thing, but many – it is defined by its repetitive publication and little else. Certainly not by its content, and increasingly not by its form. In encountering this one medium users might want to check out the latest cars or computers, financial analysis or fishing catches; they may be reaping the benefit of an expensive subscription that makes its way into bound volumes, or of assorted objects that may also be seen as artworks, or they may be inspecting a piece of junk mail that sooner rather than later will be in the bin. But what is clear is that they will want it to speak to them in a way that goes beyond the generalist nature of many magazines in the past. The thousands of new launches today involve precious few magazines aspiring to a wide audience, but instead feature very tightly focused, niche titles. And in that they aim to be so precise in reaching a particular kind of reader, the opportunity for creative diversity may actually be growing; less lowest common denominators, more opportunities to appeal to distinct character in reader groups.

Rather like the position often exhibited in contemporary art, we can see that the magazine is defined merely by the creator choosing to call it a magazine. When we speak or write of a 'magazine' we refer to a body of work past, but do not define what may come next. We have come to a definition where the magazine does not subscribe to any rules in order to be, other than the vague promise that there might be another one at some time ... that it is an issue.

Format

'The name is the only continuing factor. We don't go out of our way to change format each issue, but the themes always decide how the issue is presented.'

CECILIA DEAN, VISIONAIRE

Magazines, along with books and newspapers, remain one of the few forms of mass communication that can appear in any format their designers choose. Television images must appear in a predetermined linear order and are restricted by the standard screen space. The internet provides a slightly looser environment, but this looseness extends to the designer losing control of background colours and font choice. Magazine designers have a far freer hand in deciding what format they work in. There is no standard size, shape or extent for a magazine that will stop it functioning. A magazine can be any size and format deemed suitable. Only printing technology – the physical dimensions of the roll of paper and the printing presses – can limit the designer.

There are many different examples of magazine sizes and formats, but *Shift!* (Germany) takes experiment to its extreme, assuming a different form for each issue. Published by a group of designers in Berlin, each issue focuses on a different theme and develops the form of presentation accordingly. Issue 1 took Meat as its subject, and was presented unbound but with a hole through the corner of each page through which a meathook, supplied with the magazine, could be used as a form of binding. Issue 9 was about the art market, and consisted of a board game and CD-Rom. Such freedom is created by being self-funded, as art director and co-founder Anja Lutz explains: 'We fund it by selling it, which only works because no one involved in *Shift!* receives any payment. We also receive some material support from printers and suppliers.'

Visionaire (US) is another publication that alters its form according to the theme of each issue. 'The name is the only continuing factor. We don't go out of our way to change format each issue, but the themes always decide how the issue is presented,' explains the magazine's editor Cecilia Dean. Started in 1991, *Visionaire* is dedicated to the visual image over the word; featuring contributions from leading artists and photographers, it has become a favourite of the fashion world. Initially it was presented as a traditional printed item, albeit unbound and using many different papers. Later issues took the form of a deck of cards and a calendar, before the more recent move into yet more exotic formats: Issue 24 was the first battery-powered publication, taking the form of a lightbox with a series of pages presented as large-format transparencies. *Visionaire* is self-funded but issues such as the latter are sponsored, in that case by Gucci, whose creative director Tom Ford was the guest editor.

The more common printed magazine can appear in many more formats and sizes than a cursory glance at the shelves of your local store would suggest. The A1-sized pages of *The Manipulator* (Germany) stand at one extreme of scale. The size, chosen because its American creators 'had no other ideas', lent itself to the large-scale reproduction of art and photography by the likes of David Hockney and Bruce Weber. At the opposite extreme, and often found alongside *The Manipulator* on the shelves, was *The Fred* (UK). This A6-sized magazine, published in London during the eighties, was a compendium of various artists' drawings, poetry and prose. Coming before the advent of the Apple Mac its appearance was resolutely anti-design, its energy coming from its content rather than its layout. It remains a unique example of a small magazine.

Between these two extremes lie the more regular A4-based formats favoured by most magazines. This page size is dictated by the width of the rolls of paper and by the drum size on the web-offset printing machines used to produce mass-circulation magazines.

Paper comes in 965mm wide rolls, while the circumference of the printing press rollers limit the length of the print area to 630mm (Europe) and 578mm (US). Although recent advances in print technology have enabled designers and production staff to squeeze slightly larger pages out of the machines and rolls of paper, the limit has now been reached. The difference between European and US presses means a slight variation in each country's standard magazine format, the US version being shorter.

Magazines produced outside the mainstream can experiment further with format, however. Such magazines benefit technologically on two counts: firstly, smaller print runs mean they can print on more adaptable presses, and secondly their small-is-beautiful approach has most to gain from the computer technology that has slashed the cost of producing magazines. Ten years ago all magazines, even those published by an individual, had to be backed up by specialist services such as typesetters and repro houses. Computer technology has made it possible for one person to write the words, lay them out on the page, add scanned images, and email the pages to the printer. Magazines that might once have consisted just of xeroxed pages stapled together can now take advantage of mainstream values of production, and any such magazine is more than likely to question the usual attributes of magazines including page size and format.

Another advantage of publishing outside the mainstream is the avoidance of pressure from distributors and stores to conform to their wishes. Sales teams prefer magazines that look like magazines, that conform to the norm in other words. When Uscha Pohl, the founder and editor of *Very* (US) went to a major distributor for help she was presented with a ten-point list of ways in which she could make her magazine more marketable. The name was to run across the whole of the top of the page and fill one-third of the depth, the type should be in bright colours, the paper glossy… in short, according to this list, *Very* was the complete antithesis of the marketable magazine.

Format

There are two very different types of publishing that operate outside the mainstream: self-publishing and contract publishing. Perhaps the most extreme example of a self-published magazine playing with format is *Experiment* (UK), a London-based publication produced on a shoestring budget by a group of friends. While its content did not live up to its name, its format certainly did, being as near as possible to a round magazine. Other examples have been more practical. *Purple* (France) publishes at A5, a lack of size more than made up for by its 400+ pages. *Tank* (UK) has an even smaller page size. Both have the feel of paperback books but are clearly magazines in every other sense.

Many such projects are self-funded and survive with hardship from issue to issue. *Spoon* (US) is professionally printed but then stapled together instead of being bound. Alongside these are magazines produced with full resources backed up by a wealthy individual. *Nest* (US) appears in a normal page size but each issue features a different addition: the first two issues had a die-cut curved top right-hand corner and issue five was trimmed with a wavy right-hand edge. According to editor and art director Joseph Holtzman, these subtle additions to the look of the magazine 'stimulate creative solutions in the layouts'. He concedes that they are very expensive to produce, but explains, 'If *Nest* looks and feels good enough the reader will want to keep their issues, not throw them away.'

Choice of format also has more basic implications. The content of London listings magazine *Time Out* is primarily hard information – column after column of text. When the company launched its New York edition it did so using the shorter US page size. Publisher Tony Elliott explains that this had an advantage: '*Time Out New York* looked much more accessible than the UK edition to the reader – its smaller pages meant fewer words were presented at a time.'

Contract (or customer) magazine publishing is a relatively new area that involves producing magazines on behalf of organizations as part of their marketing campaign. British companies such as Forward Publishing and John Brown Publishing are leading the way, publishing magazines whose success is defined outside of the normal sales criteria. Instead of having to sell well to survive, they exist as part of a wider marketing and advertising strategy. This often translates into freedom for the designer.

This part of the industry is new, and has grown alongside the development of technology. The magazines produced in this sector vary enormously in quality but at their best can be very experimental and questioning of what a magazine is. As publisher John Brown points out: 'In contract publishing good design is essential. It makes the difference between success and failure.'

Colors magazine, although strictly speaking not a contract title (being produced in-house by Benetton's own team), is relevant here as it is part of Benetton's marketing strategy – it exists to aid the company's primary business, woollens. The first twelve issues of *Colors* each appeared in different formats.

In Germany, the bathroom equipment manufacturer Dornbracht has staked its reputation for good product design on the publication of a magazine, *Statements*. Again this is part of their marketing strategy, the magazine being mailed free to a list of opinion leaders, artists, editors and customers. Instead of talking directly about the company's products, the magazine features commissioned work by leading photographers such as Juergen Teller and Nick Knight. The pictures take the form of fashion shoots examining bathroom rituals, and set out to provide a context for the product. *Statements* takes the opportunity to experiment with format: the first issue was A3 while the second is a spiral-bound collection of heavily laminated pages. Issue three is a collection of video works presented in a sealed foil bag.

Back in the mainstream, it remains the case that the whole industry is geared to producing, advertising in, and distributing a certain size and format. Numerous magazines have launched in irregular formats only to revert to a more ordinary one as financial reality sets in. *Might* (US) and *Egg* (US) were both launched in a square format, arguably a far more natural shape to design with than the traditional A4 portrait-based format. Both closed, the former reverting to A4 before finally disappearing. *Mute* (UK) launched as a broadsheet newspaper before changing to a magazine format, as editor Pauline van Mourik Broekman explains: 'For advertisers, distributors and librarians, the broadsheet format was a real obstacle. It meant that *Mute* could raise only a fraction of the – already quite small – potential revenue it might raise as a new, small, unknown quarterly on art and technology.'

The Manipulator (Germany, Issue 23, 1991) 420 x 594mm Designers David Colby and Wilhelm Moser

The Fred (UK, Issue 7, 1987) 105 x 148mm Art director Unknown

Two independent magazines that experimented with scale, one A1 the other A6, shown here in proportion to each other.

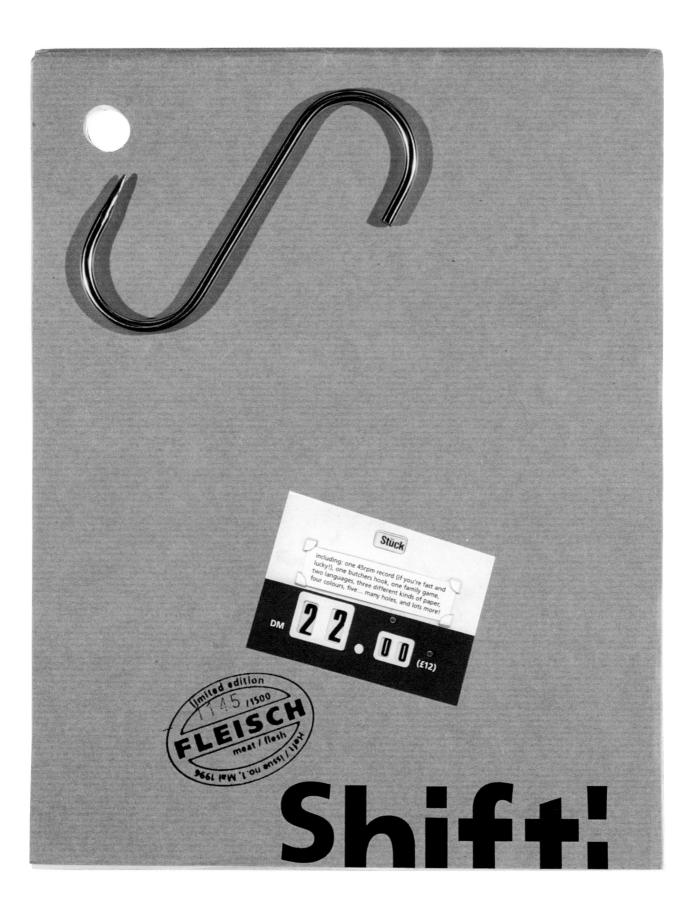

Stück

including: one 45rpm record (if you're fast and lucky!), one butchers hook, one family game, two languages, three different kinds of paper, four colours, five... many holes, and lots more!

DM 2 2 . 0 0 (£12)

limited edition
1145 /1500
FLEISCH
meat / flesh
Heft / Issue no.1, Mai 1996

Shift!

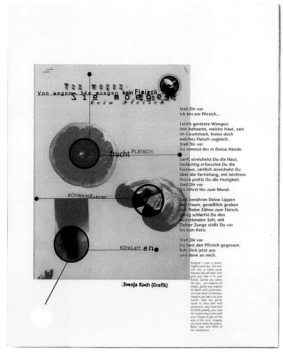

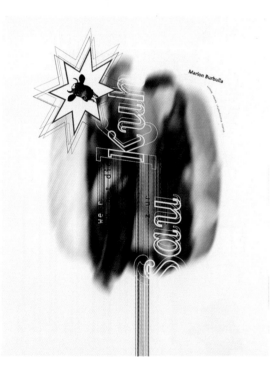

Shift! *(Germany, Issue 2, 1996) 210 x 265mm*

Shift! is published from Berlin by a group of artists and designers. Each issue has a theme, and the format alters to suit that theme; in this example the theme 'Meat' is presented as a series of loose-leaf pages held together by a butcher's meathook.

Art director Anja Lutz

UMNACHTMAHL

THEMENGEHACKTES
IN WORTSCHWALL

Schmackhaftes für
Leib und Seele!

Herzhaftes

Für Ihre
Lieben

Das Rezept für die schlagkräftige Hausfrau.

für zwei
Personen

Kochzeit
2 Stunden

Kalorien-
verbrauch
853 kcal

MARMORKUCHEN

Für größere
Gesellschaften

N

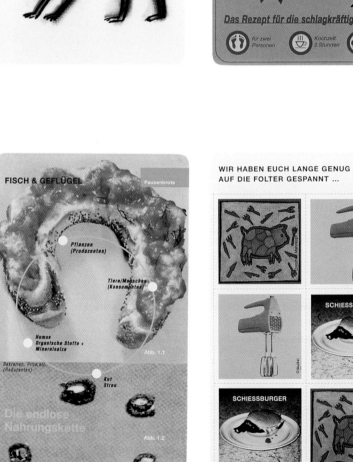

FISCH & GEFLÜGEL

Pausenbrote

Pflanzen
(Produzenten)

Tiere/Menschen
(Konsumenten)

Humus
Organische Stoffe +
Mineralsalze

Abb. 1.1

Bakterien, Pilze, etc.
(Reduzenten)

Kot
Streu

Die endlose
Nahrungskette

Abb. 1.2

WIR HABEN EUCH LANGE GENUG
AUF DIE FOLTER GESPANNT …

Pausenbrote

SCHIESSBURGER

SCHIESSBURGER

DER NEUE VON KRISEN

Aus aller Welt

E

D

F

G

NEU!

A   B

Krisen

J

C

H

Shift! (Germany, Issue 8, 1998) 200 x 130mm
This issue's theme was 'Power Games'. It took the
form of a set of cards presented in a sandwich box.
Art director Anja Lutz

VISIONAIRE 24 LIGHT
TOM FORD FOR GUCCI

A DOUBLE ISSUE

OPPOSITE **Visionaire** (*US, Issue 24, Light, 1998) 380 x 138 x 60mm*
This magazine is published in a different format every issue. For this issue the combination of the sponsorship of Gucci and the theme 'Light' led to it consisting of a black perspex box (TOP) containing a battery-powered miniature lightbox (BOTTOM). The pages were a series of large-format transparencies (CENTRE) to be viewed on the lightbox. Despite costing £300/$425 all 3,300 copies were sold, leading to this issue being considered a collector's item.
Creative director *Stephen Gan*

THIS PAGE **Visionaire** (*US, Issue 26, Fantasy, 1998) 330mm circumference*
This issue was published without sponsorship. Designed in the style of a hatbox, the theme 'Fantasy' played with the ideas of dreams and the surreal, and featured the latest haute couture collections. Inside the box was a set of loose circular pages with various interpretations of the theme, together with a fantasy mask produced by Hermès.
Creative director *Stephen Gan*
Case design *Greg Foley*

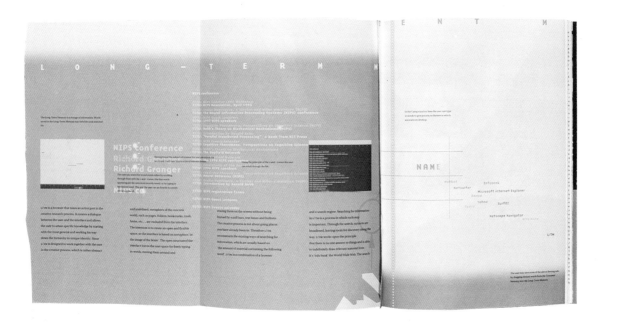

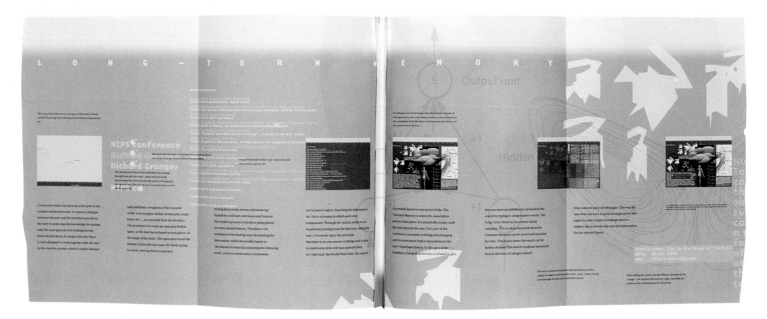

Media matic

VOL 9#2/3

Context issue

OSS/•••• by jodi

CD-ROM *for* Mac/Win

Mediamatic *(The Netherlands, Volume 9, Issue 2/3, 1998) 210 x 297mm*
This media review is published first on the internet, then as a printed edition that includes a CD-Rom. The disc is attached to page 3 and is visible through a die-cut hole in the cover. This issue is bound in such a way that many of the pages need cutting open (OPPOSITE).
Design *Ineke Bellemakers, Suzanne Grunfeld, Giselle de Oliveira, Hjordis Thorborg, Willem Velthoven*

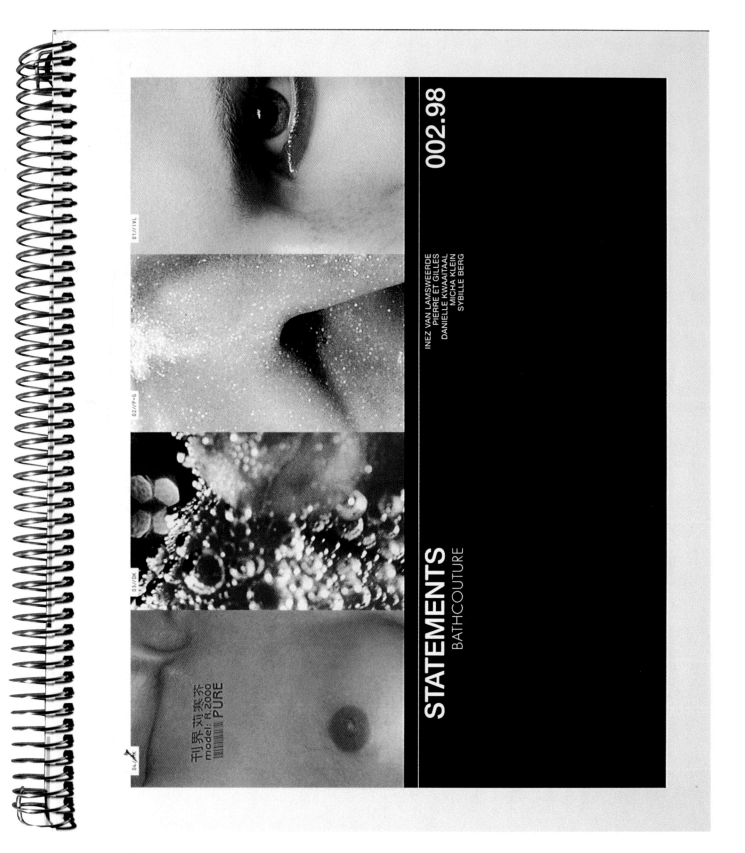

STATEMENTS
BATHCOUTURE

002.98

INEZ VAN LAMSWEERDE
PIERRE ET GILLES
DANIELLE KWAAITAAL
MICHA KLEIN
SYBILLE BERG

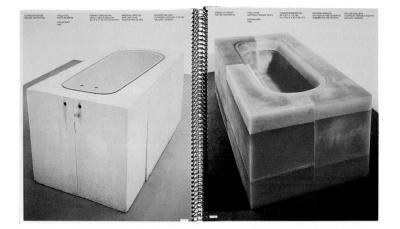

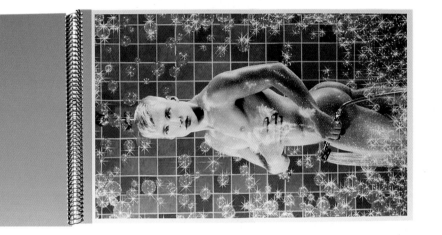

Statements *(Germany, Issue 2, 1998) 215 x 255mm*

This magazine is mailed out to customers and contacts of Dornbracht, a bathroom equipment manufacturer. Following the success of the first issue, which appeared as a tabloid, Issue 2 was produced in a more flamboyant spiral-bound format using different types of paper. Contributors include (FROM TOP) Rachel Whiteread, Pierre et Gilles and Micha Klein.

Art director *Michael Meiré*

Statements *(Germany, Issue 3, 1999)* approx. 220 x 155mm
Distributed in a sealed foil bag, the third issue of this ever-changing
magazine consists of a VHS video tape of work by artists Rosemarie Trockel,
Douglas Gordon, Lothar Hempel and Benjamin von Stuckrad-Barre.
Art directors *Michael Meiré and Brigit Reber*

Artifice *(UK, Issue 3, 1995)*
160 x 160mm
An early experiment in multimedia publishing, each issue of *Artifice* consisted of a CD-Rom and a printed magazine presented in a transparent plastic case. This combination was emphasized by repeating the central part of the magazine cover image on the front of the CD.
Design Maria Beddoes and Paul Khera

Wilde Tiere werden in vielen Kulturen gehalten und präsentiert. Häufig sind sie symbolisch bedeutsam und kursieren als Geschenke zwischen Herrschern. ‖ In Europa ist die erste nennenswerte Gefangenschaftsform wilder Tiere der Jagdpark, meist eine in der Nähe des Lustgartens liegende, eingefriedete Wildbahn. Sie hatte die Funktion, das fürstliche Jagdvergnügen zu erhöhen und heimisches oder eingebürgertes Wild verfügbar zu halten. Im Laufe der Entwicklung werden die Tiere räumlich eingegrenzt und eingestellt. Mit dem Zurücktreten der Jagd als Domäne der Versorgung entstehen Wildpark oder Tiergarten. In weitläufigen Parkanlagen werden markante Tiere immer häufiger auch zur Erbauung der Bürger in Gruppen zusammengeführt. Wisent-Gatter, Hirsch- und Sauparks, Wolfsgärten, Hirschgräben, Kanincheninseln und Fasanerien. Die Menagerien dienten der fürstlichen Repräsentation und zeigten auch vereinzelte wissenschaftliche Ambitionen an. Einzelne Löwen und Bären wurden in regelrechten Tierhäusern untergebracht, Vögel in Volieren, für Schildkröten richtete man Weiher ein und für Schnecken gab es Schreckeninseln. Von Zirkussen werden Wandermenagerien, das sind ambulante Tiersammlungen, mitgeführt oder auf Märkten ausgestellt. Die häufig dressierten Tiere bedienen die Neugier und die Schaulust. Die Tiere sind Anschauungsobjekte, mit denen sich Geld verdienen läßt. ‖ Die ersten großen zoologischen Gärten wurden im späten 18. und frühen 19. Jahrhundert in Paris, London und Amsterdam gegründet, nur wenige Jahrzehnte später folgten Gärten in den Städten kolonialisierter Länder wie Sidney, Bombay, Kalkutta, Saigon, Dschakarta, Kairo, Pretoria, aber auch in Städten unabhängiger Staaten, Tokio, Buenos Aires oder Rio de Janeiro sind hier zu nennen. ‖ In Berlin veranlaßt Friedrich Wilhelm III um 1822 die Anlage eines zoologischen Gartens auf der Pfaueninsel und im Kleinformat. Zur Ausstattung empfiehlt ihm der afrikabegeisterte Zoologe Martin Hinrich Karl Lichtenstein, der vier Jahre in Südafrika verbrachte und seit 1811 Professor der Zoologie an der Berliner Universität war, geeignete Tierarten. Friedrich Wilhelm ließ zu deren Beschaffung die Königliche Seehandlung ein Schiff nach Brasilien entsenden. Der landschaftlichen Umgestaltung der Insel nahm sich der königliche Gartendirektor Peter Joseph Lenné an. ‖ Für einen Berliner jener Zeit galt — einer Beschreibung des Dichters August Kopisch zufolge — die Fahrt zur Pfaueninsel als das schönste Familienfest des Jahres: Man träumte in Indien zu sein und sah mit einer Mischung von Lust und Grauen die exotische Tierwelt, Alligatoren und Schlangen, ja, das wunderbare Chamäleon, das opalisierend oft alle Farben der blühenden Umgebung widerzuspiegeln schien. ‖ Doch Lichtenstein wollte der Stadt näher rücken, und schon bald konkretisieren sich seine Pläne, in zentralerer Lage einen großzügigen zoologischen Garten einzurichten. In einer eigens verfaßten Schrift formuliert er einen endgültigen Abschied von den Prinzipien der Menagerie: Man ist nicht mehr zufrieden, die Muster der Tierwelt eingesperrt in enge Käfige vor sich zu sehen, man will sich an den freien Bewegungen erfreuen, man sucht nicht mehr das Grauen vor wilder Unbändigkeit, sondern das Wohlge-

fallen an schöner Gestalt und an einer befremdlicher Abweichung von dem Gewöhnlichen. ‖ Als Orientierungsmaßstab diente der Pariser JARDIN DES PLANTES und der Londoner ZOOLOGICAL GARDEN. Lichtenstein steht bezüglich dieser Pläne auch mit dem befreundeten Alexander von Humboldt in Austausch. Lenné hatte schon 1833 begonnen, einen Plan für die Umgestaltung der Fasanerie im Tiergarten zu entwerfen. Nachdem der König das die Order zur Gründung zu einer privaten Zoogesellschaft unterzeichnet hatte, begann Lenné mit der Umsetzung seiner Pläne für das gut 22 Hektar große Gelände eine geschwungene Wegführung sollte die malerisch gelegenen Tierhäuser miteinander verbinden, Strauchanlagen und durch viele Pflanzungen bereicherte Baumgruppen dem Gelände seinen Charakter geben. Friedrich Wilhelm IV, mehr der Kunst zugetan als an Beobachten von Tieren interessiert, bewilligt 1842 die Auflösung der menagerieartigen Anlagen auf der Pfaueninsel und ein großer Teil des Tierbestandes wird von der Pfaueninsel, und das zum Tiergarten gehörende Gelände der ehemaligen Fasanerie verlagert. Offizieller Zweck des Zoologischen Gartens sind neben wissenschaftlichen Beobachtungen und Untersuchungen auch künstlerische Studien sowie die Verbreitung naturhistorischer, anfänglich auch landwirtschaftlicher Kenntnisse. ‖ In Berlin war der Einrichtung des Zoos der Bau eines Naturkundemuseums vorausgegangen. Im Jahr der Gründung des Berliner Zoos bestand das Zoologische Museum der preußischen Hauptstadt bereits seit 14 Jahren. Die Sammlungen des Museums füllten in diesen Jahren bereits 12 Räume im Ostflügel des Universitätsgebäudes Unter den Linden — insgesamt 10.000 Exemplare, 90 Prozent davon waren in der jeweiligen Heimat gesammelt, 10 Prozent stammten aus den Menagerien. Im Museum war man beschäftigt, alle Tierleichen fein säuberlich zu klassifizieren und die Präparationstechniken immer weiter zu vorbessern, das heißt, mit den in dieser Zeit zügig entwickelten Techniken der Taxidermie zu behandeln, in Flüssigkeiten einzulegen oder an Bindfäden aufgehängt zu trocknen. ‖ Dem Zoo — bald in der Rechtsform einer Aktiengesellschaft — wird anfänglich mit Skepsis begegnet. Die Anteile verkaufen sich schlecht, und grassierende Seuchen dezimieren den Tierbestand immer wieder erheblich. Zudem machen sich Besucher einen Spaß daraus, die Tiere zu traktieren und mit ungeeignetem Futter zu versorgen. Ernst Dronke kritisiert den hohen Eintrittspreis von fünf Silbergroschen und kommentiert: In dem großen Park kann man sehr bedeutende Strecken weit wandern, bevor man an einen neuen Behälter kommt; der ganze Inhalt aber beschränkt sich auf einige Affen, welche sich um einen großen Baum herumbalgen, zwei Bären, einige fremde Vögel und sonst mehrere Tiere. Über deren Käfig die Worte aus hiesiger Gegend zu lesen sind. Die ärmlichste Menagerie eines auf den Jahrmärkten der Provinz umherziehenden Marktschreiers ist besser als diese erbärmliche Anstalt. ‖ Neuerwertungen in den fünfziger Jahren ziehen zeitweise immer wieder ein größeres Publikumsinteresse nach sich. Inzwischen hatte sich ein differenzierter Tiermarkt herausgebildet, für attraktiv befundene exotische Tiere konnten gezielt eingekauft werden. Ab 1869 wurde die Landschaftsgestaltung tiefgreifenden Revisionen unterzogen: das Gelände wurde erweitert, und der 89

reparatur ist kein vorgang bloßen wiederingangsetzens. reparatur ist eine konsequenz kultureller erfahrung, eine kumulation kulturellen kapitals. gegenwärtig gibt es auf der welt insgesamt noch etwa 500 historische lauten. lauten also, die älter sind als ungefähr 300 jahre. die lebensdauer eines solchen instruments beträgt seinerzeit allerdings nur 10 jahre. immer wieder wurden die fragilen instrumente repariert, späterhin infolge veränderten musikgeschmacks auch modifiziert und umgebaut, bis dann eine andere musikkultur andere instrumente an deren stelle setzte. zu seiner blütezeit galt das lautenmachen als höchste kunst und noch heute werden in frankreich instrumentenmacher *luthiers* genannt. dieser text entsteht aus der begegnung mit dem lautenmacher johannes georg boucken als versuch, das reparieren als einen kulturellen vorgang in langen zeitlichen dimensionen anzuschreiben und die frage wachzurufen, welche kompetenzen, welche hör-, seh- und fühlweisen historisch bereits gebildet sind gegenüber gegenständen in der sinnlichen dimension von körper und hand.

5

Form + Zweck *(Germany, Issue 11/12, 1994) 210 x 313mm*
Started in 1956 in the GDR as a state-run publication to 'discuss the cultural functions of industrial design in a socialist state', *Form + Zweck* (Form + Purpose) had to redefine itself following the re-unification of Germany in 1989. In doing so it rejected standard magazine formats, choosing not to compete with the newly available Western publications. Instead it uses different formats, papers and binding methods for each issue. This example is bound with metal studs through punched holes to illustrate the theme 'Repair'. In addition, every page apart from the front cover is perforated by a set of nine holes.
Design Cyan

Issue 1, Summer 1997

Issue 3, Winter 1998/9

Nest (US) 230 x 280mm
While always having the same page size, each issue of this independent interiors magazine changes its presentation slightly. The first two issues appeared with a die-cut curved top right corner; Issue 3 had a wrap-around cloth banner; Issue 5 had a die-cut wavy right edge; once bound, Issue 6 had four small holes drilled right through it.
Art director *Joseph Holtzman*

Issue 6, Autumn 1999

Issue 5, Summer 1999

in
juve

JORDI **V**ILLACAMPA

OLÍMPICOS E **S**PAÑOLES

Revista del Instituto
de la Juventud

Junio 1991 | Número 9 | Precio 200 ptas.

MÚSICA EN 62   LÍNEAS

BER   ÍN

SY   ILLA

ANT   NIO MUÑOZ MOLINA

DAVID SUMMERS

Hijo de padre famoso, mimado por una vida sin mayores problemas, David Summers, es la cara de Hombres G. Su sueño era grabar un disco, pero hoy el éxito le acompaña aunque no se lo proponga. La causa, según él, es que dejó de ser un mal estudiante para convertirse en un buen músico.

MÚSICA
EN 625 LÍNEAS

Eran los tiempos en los que en la pequeña pantalla comenzaron a asomarse una serie de músicas distintas destinadas a deleitar a un incipiente grupo de adictos a la música moderna, músicas, que bajo el común denominador de ser visionadas en blanco y negro, excepto para aquellos afortunados que ya disponían de receptor en color, eran la temática principal de una serie de programas que rompían una lanza en favor de otra clase de música más subversiva que la que escuchaban nuestros padres.

OLÍMPICOS ESPAÑOLES
PREPARADOS
LISTOS
YA!

Han dejado atrás su niñez y media adolescencia en pos de un objetivo, y su vida supo desde temprano de horarios, restricciones y disciplina. Abrazan el deporte como una pasión y se entregan a él sin condicionamientos. Con la vista puesta en los XXV Juegos Olímpicos de Barcelona 92, le encuentran cada vez más sabor a la carrera, a la velocidad, al salto, a la precisión... Ellos serán los protagonistas.

In Juve
(Spain, Issue 9, 1991)
200 x 400mm
A good example of how an alternative format can be exploited: the cut-out figure on the cover suits its long shape well, while the design of the pages inside makes the most of the square shape of the opened spreads.
Design SUMMA

Petit Glam style culture fashion

no. 3

Dick Bruna Special

Lance Wyman

Tropicalia of Latin Sound

Cris Moor + Thuy Pham

Takashi Homma

Kenshu Shintsubo

Keiko Okumura

Motoko + groovisions

<The Separate Volume> Petit Glam Artist Book Series
White Book by Tam Ochiai

Paradise in **Pictograms** Issue

Style Culture Fashion Petit Glam N° 3 1998 **Groovy Trends for Glamour People** Petit Grand Publishing

Illustrations Dick Bruna, ©copyright Mercis b.v., 1997

Petit Glam *(Japan, Issue 3, 1998) 180 x 130mm*
This magazine, aimed at young Japanese designers
and design students, is published at a very small size
and presented in a plastic dust-jacket in order to
stand apart from other magazines in the market.
Art director *Takaya Goto*

PURPLE

NUMBER 2 · 75 F $14 · WINTER 98 99
FASHION PROSE FICTION INTERIORS AND MORE

BEAUTY BY
BERNADETTE VAN-HUY AND KATJA RAHLWES

PHOTOGRAPHS KATJA RAHLWES
MAKE-UP BERNADETTE VAN-HUY
MODEL PAMELA AICH (IMG)
HAIR PIECE KEVIN WOON
GRAY SUEDE JACKET BRUCE
PRINTS MARC UPSON
BEAUTY PRODUCTS MAC

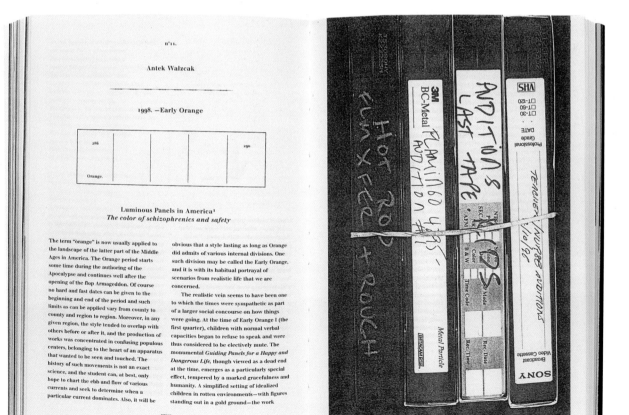

n°11.

Antek Walzcak

———————————————

1998. – Early Orange

288					290
Orange.					

Luminous Panels in America[1]
The color of schizophrenics and safety

The term "orange" is now usually applied to the landscape of the latter part of the Middle Ages in America. The Orange period starts some time during the authoring of the Apocalypse and continues well after the opening of the flop Armageddon. Of course no hard and fast dates can be given to the beginning and end of the period and such limits as can be applied vary from county to county and region to region. Moreover, in any given region, the style tended to overlap with others before or after it, and the production of works was concentrated in confusing populous centers, belonging to the heart of an apparatus that wanted to be seen and touched. The history of such movements is not an exact science, and the student can, at best, only hope to chart the ebb and flow of various currents and seek to determine when a particular current dominates. Also, it will be obvious that a style lasting as long as Orange did admits of various internal divisions. One such division may be called the Early Orange, and it is with its habitual portrayal of scenarios from realistic life that we are concerned.

The realistic vein seems to have been one to which the times were sympathetic as part of a larger social concourse on how things were going. At the time of Early Orange I (the first quarter), children with normal verbal capacities began to refuse to speak and were thus considered to be electively mute. The monumental *Guiding Panels for a Happy and Dangerous Life*, though viewed as a dead end at the time, emerges as a particularly special effect, tempered by a marked gracefulness and humanity. A simplified setting of idealized children in rotten environments—with figures standing out in a gold ground—the work

prose

Purple (*France, Issue 2, Winter 1998/99) 155 x 212mm*
This paperback-sized magazine, shown real size (OPPOSITE), is actually several different magazines in one: *Purple Fashion* (THIS PAGE, TOP) is printed on glossy paper and consists of 176 pages of cutting edge fashion photography. *Purple Prose*, (THIS PAGE, BELOW) uses a cream coloured matt paper stock and features a series of essays about colour. This issue also contains *Purple Fiction* and *Purple Interiors.*
Art directors *Ellen Fleiss and Christopher Brunnquell*

A square format is an easy way to stand out from the competition, but can also cause distribution and store display problems. Neither *Egg* nor *Might* lasted long before ceasing publication, the latter even tried changing to a more regular format before closing. *Spoon* remains square and is printed as a set of single pages held together by heavy-duty staples. As a small print-run printed version of a website it can avoid the normal commercial pressures. As a contract magazine produced on behalf of Ikea, *Room* can avoid these pressures too.

experiment

Experiment *(UK, 1995) 180mm circumference*
The need for a straight edge for binding leaves
the left side slightly mis-shapen, but otherwise a
unique attempt at producing a circular magazine.
Designer *Mike Lawrence*

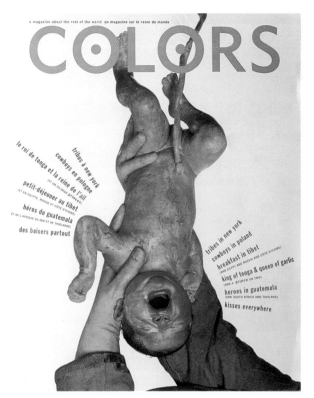

Issue 1, 280 x 350mm

Issue 2, 358 x 552mm

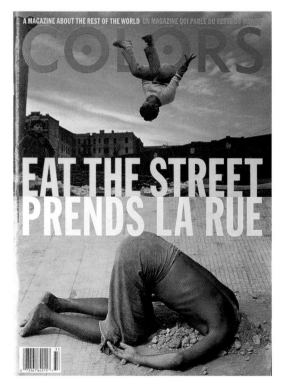

Issue 5, 250 x 345mm

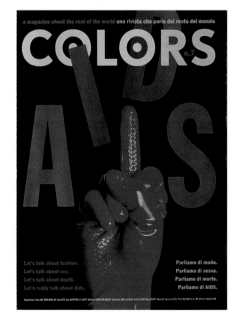

Issue 7, 194 x 270mm

Issue 3, 290 x 470mm

Issue 4, 285 x 305mm

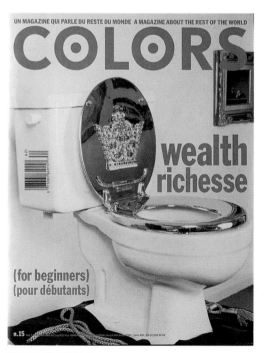

Issue 15, 230 x 300mm

Colors *(Italy)*

Initially each issue of *Colors* was produced to a different format. By Issue 14 the page size was always one of two formats – either 230 x 287mm or 230 x 300mm.

Editor-in-chief *Tibor Kalman*

Art directors *Emily Oberman (1); Paul Ritter (3, 4, 5); Scott Stowell (7); Paul Ritter, Leslie Mello and Meg Kimmel (15)*

TOP **Mute** *(UK, Issue 5, 1996) 405 x 575mm*

BOTTOM **Mute** *(UK, Issue 9, 1997) 200 x 275mm*

Two years after i:s launch as a broadsheet format newspaper,
Mute reinvented itself as a magazine – a case of advertising and
distribution requirements dictating format.
Design Damion Jacques

Blow *(UK)*

'It was anti-fashion, anti-design, anti-everything that was on at the time. Anti-glossy.'

MICHAEL OLIVEIRA-SALAC

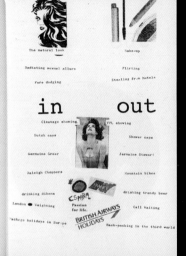

The natural look   Make-up

Radiating sexual allure   Flirting

Fare dodging   Stealing from hotels

in   out

Cleavage showing   VPL showing

Dutch caps   Shower caps

Germaine Greer   Jermaine Stewart

Raleigh Choppers   Mountain bikes

drinking Ribena   drinking trendy beer

London • Weighting   Passion for life.   Call Waiting

Package holidays in Europe   BRITISH AIRWAYS HOLIDAYS   Back-packing in the third world

---

ENJOY OUR MAGNIFICENT REVIEW OF THE OUTFITS WORN BY IVANA TRUMP IN THAILAND

IVANA TRUMP IN GLITZ AND GLAMOUR

TALKS ABOUT HER PAINFUL MARRIAGE BREAK-UP

Jacket and Pants: Red or Dead

Denise & pink frizzed bikini - Bella trend

---

suzy's sex tips for
boys

Call me stupid. The penny was a long time in dropping, but the realisation has finally dawned: this column has been addressing entirely the wrong audience. Sex tips for girls? Stupid, stupid, stupid.

In fashionable circles there is in operation a cruel and vicious double standard. A lady with dress sense is intelligent, sophisticated, discerning, and an absolute demon in bed. Such a girl does not need advice on how to conduct herself between the sheets. Her male counterparts, however, are invariably shallow and vacuous, drugged out and absolutely devoid of manners; and truly appalling in bed.

What is to be done? Will we end up sacrificing fashion for sex? Will we have to go cruising at The Limelight instead of Billion Dollar Babes?

There now follows a last-ditch attempt to educate our menfolk: Suzy's Sex Tips For Boys. Bearing is mind that they are all superficial creatures, it will perhaps be best to present these tips in terms of what is "in" and what is "out". In other words, tell him that cunnilingus is extremely fashionable, and you might get lucky.

* * * * * * *

molotto

QUALITY TURNS

COAST

---

clubreview

AT THE Cafe de Paris

Tries to get the girls on top, but, as usual, attract the cruisy men in eighties revival mode - or have they just not realised that this is the nineties?

Peach dress – Comme des garçons
leather bustier, cream muslin shirt and black wrap – Beauty & Beast by PIL

Blow was started in 1993 by two students, James Pretlove and Michael Oliveira-Salac. They knew each other through the London club scene, and inspired by New York magazine *Rome* they decided to try and publish a scrapbook record of their time clubbing before getting down to serious college work. 'We thought London needed something that documented what was happening in the clubs but did not take itself too seriously.' So they put together the first issue of *Blow* and printed 350 copies.

Their aim was to poke fun at those who took themselves too seriously. Each issue had lengthy In and Out lists, sending up London's fashion victims. Issue 1 featured over 40 full-page pictures of Linda Evangelista simply xeroxed out of other magazines. An interview with the band Suede was illustrated with items found in the lead singer's flat – his toothbrush, the gas bill and other personal

items. It was anarchic in an exciting and positive way.

Through the interest of a fashion PR word spread about the new project, and suddenly this scrapbook was discussed as a magazine. 'We never intended it to be a magazine, but it became a kind of trade magazine' explains Oliveira-Salac. 'PRs, ad agency creatives, design students, all sorts of people who consume magazines were buying it.'

What they got was about a hundred sheets of A4 paper printed in black and white on one side and bound using an office binding machine. As this basic format indicates, at the magazine's heart was an ethos of do-it-yourself. Oliveira-Salac and Pretlove did all the work, editing and distributing it round London. 'It is a decadent hobby running any form of magazine,' explains Oliveira-Salac. 'Getting it printed and out into the shops takes a lot of effort and I respect that. Even if the magazine

is shit, I respect the people doing it. I take my hat off to anyone who publishes a first issue, but it's issues two and three I really respect.'

Blow continued for twelve issues, closing just before Issue 13 was due to go to press. By then the format had developed, slowly taking on the appearance of a regular magazine. Sponsorship from Smirnoff led to it being perfect bound (the sponsor wanted their logo on the spine), and colour covers were introduced. Oliveira-Salac explains 'You've got no choice. Advertisers will say they want you to be independent and different but they don't really, because of their big clients. They want to be in, but when they see the magazine and the way it looks they change their mind.' This wasn't an unwelcome pressure, though. 'It got better and better. Issue 13 was going to be full colour, but we were under-resourced. We would look at other magazines and think "if only we had their resources".'

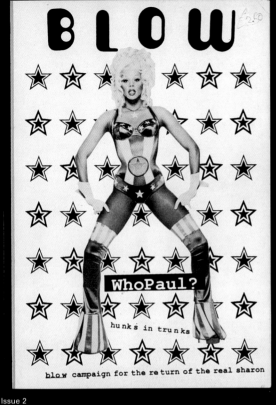

Issue 2

Issue 6

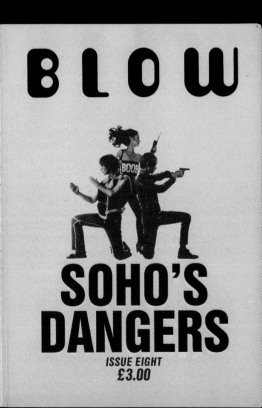

Issue 8

Issue 11

As the magazine developed, the front cover became more commercial and sophisticated.

Covers

'The problem with covers is you end up trying to catch the floating readers. You ignore the 100,000 who buy the magazine every month and target the 200,000 who occasionally buy it.'

ROBIN DERRICK, VOGUE UK

It has always been the case that covers have to sell magazines to the reader; they act as a poster attracting the reader from across the store. It is only with the growth in the industry and consequent competition, however, that covers have developed into full-on marketing tools, and nowhere more so than in the world's biggest magazine market, America.

The US edition of *Vogue* is a good example of this; every cover is planned meticulously. Ex-art director of US *Vogue* Sheila Jack explains: 'Sometimes we would do two or three shoots for a cover, all very similar, often using the same model and same clothes. The editor would insist on having the latest piece of clothing Concorded in from Paris.' Certain types of girl would sell a cover. The ideal US *Vogue* cover featured all-American girl Cindy Crawford against a blue-sky background. Since this could not be repeated every issue it was saved for issues that research showed were hard to sell, such as the February and August ones, which immediately preceded the issues featuring the new fashion collections.

Other covers would feature those supermodels that research showed to be perceived as less 'all-American girl', that is, too cool and European. Models such as Linda Evangelista were given a makeover to appear warmer and hence more 'American'. Hair would be softened and a big smile encouraged. All this from a magazine that has a relatively easy target to hit. *Vogue*, in all the twelve countries in which it publishes, has a reputation that precedes it. The cover has to sell the new issue rather than the whole concept of the magazine.

The sales function of magazine covers in general can be divided into two sometimes conflicting parts: the cover has to sell the idea of the magazine as a whole – be it a woman's

fashion magazine or a film magazine, for example – while at the same time expressing the fact that this is a new issue of that particular magazine. The cover has to shout to the casual reader that this magazine is about X, while also addressing both casual and regular readers and explaining the content of that particular issue.

The strongest example of this conflict is found on weekly titles. An issue of a weekly magazine will be on display in stores until the end of one day, only to be replaced by the new issue the very next. The covers of such magazines have to be reassuringly familiar so as to be recognizable, whilst also being different enough for the reader to realize that the issue on sale is a new one. Thus magazines such as *Newsweek*, *The Economist* and *Time Out* have heavily formatted cover designs that rely on strong mastheads and constant devices such as, in the case of *Newsweek*, a thick red border round the cover image. At the same time, these magazines use the picture area of their covers to be as different week-on-week as possible. They will use every variation: one week illustration, the next photography; one week predominately blue, the next predominately yellow; one week a celebrity, the next an abstract concept.

Whatever the changing content of a cover may include, the key component is the title – both the actual name and the design that presents it. Given time, a magazine title will become an entity in its own right. Titles like *Vogue*, *Esquire* and *GQ* have outgrown both their original meaning and typefaces and become brands, complete with copyright tags. Few readers stop to think what the words 'Vogue' or 'Esquire' actually mean; they pick up the magazines of those names recognizing the masthead design. This relationship between the name, the design of the name and

the content of the magazine must be accurate; the title designs of *Vogue* and *Esquire* both show this – the delicate serifs of *Vogue* and the chunky handwritten *Esquire* both reflect their respective markets. The name, the design and the relationship between the two are all equally important in creating a magazine title.

However, first the magazine needs a good name. The original trio of British style magazines were all started independently at the beginning of the eighties. They all took names that attempted to relate to contemporary British youth culture, and did so with varying success: *i-D* was the standard abbreviation for identity; *The Face* was the Mod name for the trend leader; *Blitz* took the name of a nightclub. The former two were always going to be timeless, the latter would inevitably fall out of favour.

In the far less competitive market earlier this century, magazines were able to sell on their name only – adding additional copy to a cover was considered unneccesary. These days most magazine covers are smothered in coverlines shouting to attract the potential buyer. And the strategy works, as Robin Derrick, art director of British *Vogue*, has pointed out. 'The problem with covers,' he explains, 'is that you end up trying to catch the floating readers. You ignore the 100,000 who buy the magazine every month and target the 200,000 who buy it occasionally. You end up trying to pitch to people passing through train stations.' Derrick's favourite *Vogue* cover remains the Kate Moss cover shown on page 58. 'We picked Kate for the cover but didn't want it to be a fashion cover, so I commissioned Nick Knight to do this headshot. It was that rare cover where everything all fell into place and everyone loved it from the moment it was shot. I love its simplicity and purity.'

Covers

In a general sense all magazines look remarkably similar: a set of ad-hoc rules has developed to help them fulfil their marketing obligations. The logo always runs across the top of the page; a life-size face with eye contact attracting the reader is deemed essential. As many of the stories as possible should be featured as headlines and teasers. It is these unofficial guidelines – the received wisdom of how to design a successful magazine – that lead to the many similarities across mainstream magazines. Alongside these broad rules are the specific, local rules – those dictated by individual editors and publishers. Over-generalized statements such as 'covers featuring green won't sell', and more insidiously, 'black people on covers don't sell' proliferate as publishers attempt to account for variations in sales.

The growth in competition has also meant the pictorial content of covers has become much more limited. Mainstream magazines now almost exclusively feature full-colour headshots. Publishers are forever looking over their shoulders to see what their rivals are doing, and any successful idea is endlessly copied. The recent success in the UK of the men's magazines *FHM* and *Maxim* has led their competitors to rush to copy their semi-clad starlet cover formula. With the launch of *Maxim* that same formula is beginning to succeed in the US. *Details*, *GQ*, *Gear*, *Bikini* – magazines with a predominately male readership – are all following this trend.

Other factors come into play. Some magazines cannot afford to use photography and have to find alternative ways of selling themselves. An example of working to a tight budget successfully was David King's powerful series of covers for the launch of the left-wing listings magazine *City Limits* (UK). Drawing on the typographical style of the Russian Constructivists, King took advantage of the small budget to produce a very strong graphic approach that immediately gave the new magazine its own look and feel. Its oppositional political stance was well expressed by the primary colours and graphic devices used; the logo would change colour, size and position, sometimes taking up the whole of the cover.

David King's covers were published twenty years ago. Opposing the mainstream remains a valid option for many magazines, but now the market is not oppositional politics. Instead it is youth culture, or oppositional fashion. David Carson's covers for *Raygun* (US) turned many conventions on their heads. Why should the masthead always be presented in the same typeface and in the same position? For a period each issue of Raygun featured a different design for its masthead. The coverlines featured the usual list of contents but would include the words 'new masthead'.

Raygun subsequently settled on a regular masthead, but not before its influence had affected a host of magazines. While Carson went on to produce perhaps the most extremely illegible masthead yet for *Speak* magazine (US), New York's *Paper* magazine created a different version of its masthead every issue.

Away from the overtly commercial area of mainstream publishing, the designer is freer still to experiment with covers. When London club *SleazeNation* started its own magazine it took the oblique approach to its extreme. Each cover featured a different photograph on which some existing type had been altered to read *SleazeNation*. Obscurity was the point. But that reflected the nature of the magazine. As a small-scale, free publication available in clubs and bars around the city it could afford this deliberate anti-hard-sell stance. It has since relaunched as a paid-for title and has become increasingly conventional with each issue (see page 53).

Taking obscurity even further, issue E of *A Be Sea* (UK) featured a blank white cover. This arts magazine, financed and published as a labour of love by Sebastian Boyle, was published irregularly during the early nineties and distributed free through art galleries and bars in London. 'Conceptually the blank cover was great, but it didn't help sales', explains Boyle. 'I was ready to sell out, to go all commercial, but my contributors wouldn't let me.'

There are also some mainstream areas where the hard sell is less essential. Newspaper supplements have been sold to the reader as part of an overall package since the sixties, and bought without the supplement cover being seen. In the US every self-respecting newspaper publishes a magazine-format supplement each weekend, while in Europe tabloid-sized supplements have provided designers such as Vince Frost, Mark Porter and Fernando Gutiérrez with the opportunity to design covers removed from the commercial reality of news-stand titles.

Gutiérrez art directed the *El Pais* (Spain) supplement *Tentaciones* ('Temptations'). The covers had a very set style: 'I couldn't bleed the pictures due to the way it was being printed, but by using cut-out pictures it looked like the images were bleeding off.' The masthead ran across the image, but not always in the same position. 'If the image needed it, I could run the masthead across the bottom of the cover, I could be playful with it. You're not selling it in a store – the magazine came inside the paper.'

Arena, Esquire, FHM, GQ, Loaded *(UK, August 1998)* The summer 1998 issues of these men's magazines try to out-sex each other with their covers.

RAY GUN

music + style
(the bible of)

issue #3, featuring :

dinosaur jr.

shamen, screaming
trees, flaming lips,
michael stipe, shabba
ranks, new logo, the
orb, etc.

U.S.A.
$3.50

CAN.
$3.95

FEB 1993   £ 2.50
02

5 021616 108008
COMAG

Issue 3, February 1993

Issue 4, March 1993

Issue 5, April 1993

Issue 9, September 1993

Issue 10, October 1993

Issue 11, November 1993

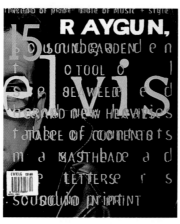

Issue 15, April 1994

Issue 21, November 1994

Issue 20, October 1994

Issue 24, March 1995

Issue 26, May 1995

Raygun (US) 255 x 305mm
Setting out to break as many of the established rules as possible, *Raygun* even altered its logo from issue to issue.
Art director *David Carson*

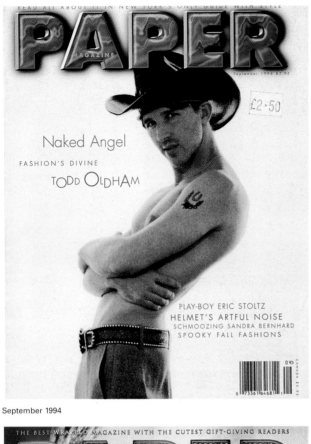

September 1994

November 1994

December 1997

June 1998

Paper *(US)* 218 x 275mm
While the logo always runs in the same typeface and position, for each issue a different effect is applied to it.
Art director *Brigit de Socio*

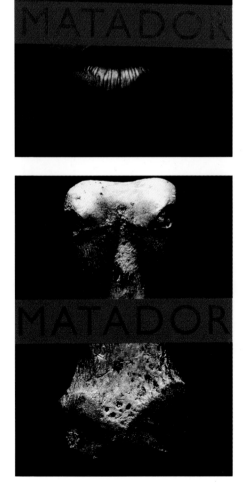

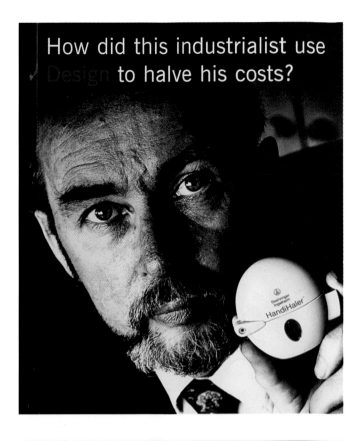

Matador *(Spain, Issue A, 1995; Issue B, 1996; Issue C, 1997) 300 x 415mm*

Sold by subscription only, and published only once a year, *Matador* enjoys the luxury of not having to use the cover to sell itself. Instead the covers feature striking but relatively abstract black and white photography, with no type or masthead. Its title is printed on a red wrap-around band.

Art director Fernando Gutiérrez

Design *(UK, Spring 1995, Spring 1996) 230 x 280mm*

This has no logo as such – the title of the magazine is picked out of the single coverline.

Art director Quentin Newark

Post-Acid *(Spain, 1989) 240 x 320mm*
Constructing the masthead and type around the image,
this cover breaks the rule of masthead-at-the-top.
Art director *Stephen Male*

Blah Blah Blah *(UK, Issue 1, April 1996) 230 x 300mm*
The masthead on this music magazine was designed to be adaptable, the layout of the
three 'Blahs' varying each time to suit the composition of the picture and other type.
Art directors *Chris Ashworth and Neil Fletcher*
Photograph *Phil Poynter*

Plazm *(US, Issue 14, 1996; Issue 17, 1998; Issue 19, 1998) 230 x 303mm*
Every cover of this magazine is commissioned from a different
designer, meaning no continuity or link from issue to issue.
Art directors *Joshua Berger, Niko Courtelis and Pete McCracken*
Cover designs, from top: Issue 14 by *Rick Valicenti/Thirst*; Issue 17
by *Ed Fella*; Issue 19 by *Rebecca Mendez and Jorge Verdin*

#CAR-RT SORT++++++$7.95
#EMIGRE00000000041 FEB97

EMIGRE NO. 41
THE MAGAZINE ISSUE
WINTER   1997
PRICE$7.95

Emigré *(US, Issue 41, Winter 1997) 210 x 285mm*

Originally produced in large format, design theory magazine *Emigré* changed to A4. With the format change the covers became more obtuse, abandoning their regular logo and instead using the cover to illustrate the theme of the issue. In this example an issue about magazine design features a dark photograph of a designer's work station, while what type there is mimics a magazine subscription postage label.

Designer Rudy VanderLans

World Cup semi-final
tickets to be won

World Cup wallchart
Alan McGee
Why everything you've been
told about fashion is wrong
Mark Lamarr
Homegrown cinema
Elodie Bouchez
£3.60/$6.00

LONGNECK#2

Budweiser

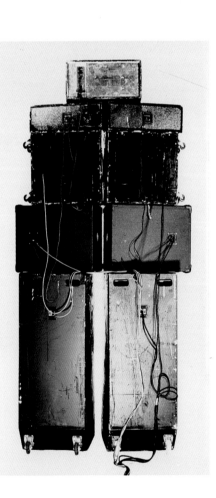

Adrian Sherwood
Cornelius
Bill Bailey
Chloé Sevigny
Canice Lambe
Psycho Panda
£3.60/$6.00

LONGNECK#3

Budweiser

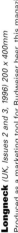

Longneck (UK, Issues 2 and 3, 1996) 200 x 400mm
Produced as a marketing tool for Budweiser beer, this magazine can ignore some of the commercial demands of front covers. The logo and coverlines are played down and a photographic style used to help recognition. The objects in the pictures refer in a general sense to the content of the issue (sport, music) and as there was no advertising the back covers were used to develop the imagery.
Art director *Jeremy Leslie*
Photographer *Richard Dean*

Issue 4, February 1997

Issue 5, March 1997

Issue 8, June 1997

Issue 12, October 1997

SleazeNation (UK) 190 x 238mm

When it was still a free magazine distributed around clubs and bars in London, *SleazeNation* ran front covers consisting of an image containing a small piece of type doctored to read SleazeNation.

Art directors *Tristan Dellaway and Martin Tickner*

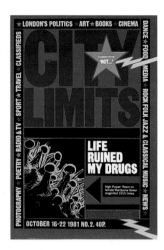

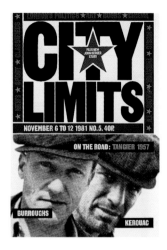

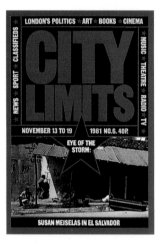

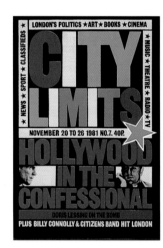

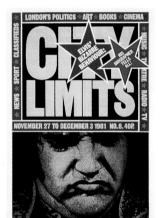

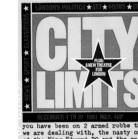

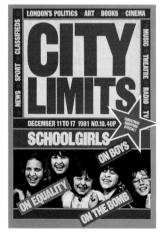

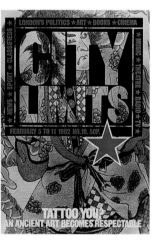

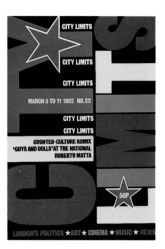

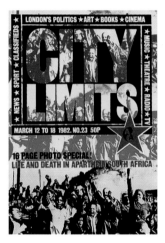

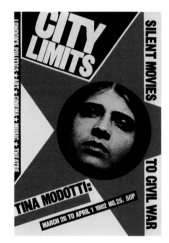

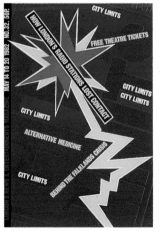

City Limits (UK, 1981, 1982)
210 x 300mm

The magazine cover as poster: lacking the money for photo shoots, this weekly listings magazine relied on David King's Constructivist type and graphics to produce an extraordinarily strong and ever-changing identity. The size and position of the logo constantly altered, but the use of just one typeface and a limited set of colours meant the covers were instantly recognizable.

Art director *David King*

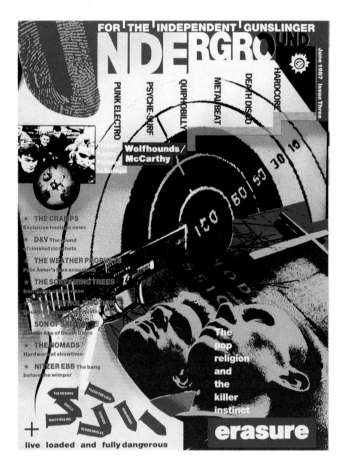

Underground *(UK, Issue 3, June 1987) 210 x 280mm*
Using some of the same references that inspired David King's covers for *City Limits*, this rock magazine combined text and image on its covers in a way that foresaw what the Apple Mac was soon to do.
Designer Rod Clark

A Be Sea *(UK, 1992) 270 x 380mm*
The first issue of this arts magazine was called A; later issues proceeded alphabetically as far as J. Each cover dealt with its title in a different way: Issue A used bold typography, while Issue C used a visual pun, featuring a picture of the sea.
Designer Sebastian Boyle

SPECIAL 5TH ANNIVERSARY ISSUE

WIRED

¡Conéctate!   January 1998

CHANGE IS GOOD

The State
of the Planet
1998
Joey Anuff
John Perry Barlow
Po Bronson
John Browning
George Gilder
Danny Hillis
Jaron Lanier
Oliver Morton
Nicholas Negroponte
Virginia Postrel
Randall Rothenberg
Julian Simon
Steve G. Steinberg
Bruce Sterling

£3.95

Conversations about the future   October/November 1996 £3.50

FILTER

9 770037 480038   08

Crime: Is crime caused by social justice, or are criminals just plain evil? Maybe neither. Maybe crime is an epidemic. And if it is, we know how to wipe it out. **Page 48**

Cities: What will the city of the future look like? Does it already exist? We look at three contenders. Two are being formed by left-wing regimes. The other by Disney. **Page 34**

Ads: Pepsi spent £350 million turning blue. Why? Because as products get more and more alike, they're not sold on features anymore –just on their colour. **Page 42**

Time: "How soon is now?" asked The Smiths. "Good question," say The Clock Library. Will a giant clock in a desert help cure the world of short-termism? **Page 54**

Weather: Is global warming just a big myth? Yes it is, according to a new report. **Page 62**

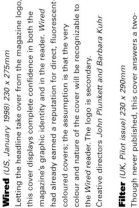

Wired *(US, January 1998) 230 x 275mm*
Letting the headline take over from the magazine logo, this cover displays complete confidence in both the magazine's graphic identity and in the reader. *Wired* had already earned a reputation for direct, fluorescent-coloured covers; the assumption is that the very colour and nature of the cover will be recognizable to the *Wired* reader. The logo is secondary.
Creative directors *John Plunkett and Barbara Kuhr*

Filter *(UK. Pilot issue) 230 x 290mm*
Though never published, this cover answers a two-way brief to not look like any other magazine yet still be commercial. While there is no cover image, the logo and bands of colour give the design a strong visual identity; the detailed description of what is inside acts almost as an immediate contents list.
Designer *Mark Porter*

VOGUE

JUNE
£2.90

SPECIAL
ISSUE

BEST OF BRITISH

HOT, HAPPENING AND HERE

Vogue *(UK, June 1998) 220 x 285mm*
Model Kate Moss was chosen for the cover of a special issue
celebrating British style. To signify that the issue was not dealing
with fashion alone the picture was taken as a close-up headshot, a
rare choice for *Vogue*. Equally rare is the relative lack of coverlines.
Art director *Robin Derrick*
Photographer *Nick Knight*

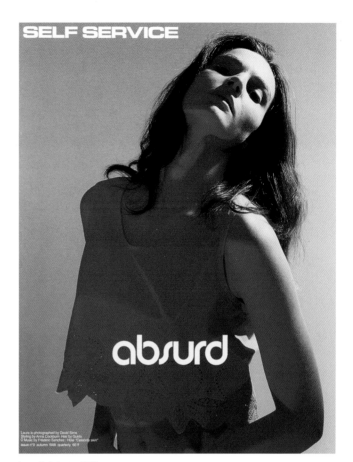

Issue 6, Autumn/Winter 1997

Issue 9, Autumn 1998

Issue 10, Spring 1999

Self Service *(France) 230 x 300mm*
Consisting almost exclusively of fashion photography, this magazine is distributed and sold through galleries and fashion stores. As such its covers do not have to compete on the news-stand and so can ignore the usual rules. Instead they feature a fashion image with a headline announcing the title or theme of the issue.
Creative director Ezra Petronio
Art direction Work In Progress

Issue 1, August 1997

Issue 2, November 1997

Issue 4, August 1998

Issue 5, December 1998

Very *(US) 215 x 280mm*
Published from a New York gallery space, this magazine sets out to promote collaboration and help artists and designers present their ideas. It is resolutely non-commercial in its approach; the name Very is deliberately vague, describing nothing but applicable to everything. The one constant is the cover image which is always a photograph by Angela Hill of a young woman. These are not models; for most of the women it is their first time in front of a professional photographer's camera. They represent the fresh nature of the magazine while also mocking the standard cover shot of a famous person.
Art director Angela Hill

Blag *(UK, Issues 8,9,10, 1997/8) 215 x 280mm*
This magazine is all about attitude. Started by sisters Sally and Sarah Edwards while at art college in 1992, it has an uncompromising approach that is epitomized by these covers – with no text or explanation, they aim to attract through intrigue; you either get it or you don't.
Design Yacht Associates

VISUAL \ CULTURE \ DOCUMENT   VOL 1 : NO 1

2wice

feet

VISUAL \ CULTURE \ DOCUMENT   VOL 2 : NO 1

2wice

SELF

DR. IAN WILMUT   MAYA ANGELOU   LEWIS BLACK   SUSAN DER

VISUAL \ CULTURE \ DOCUMENT   VOL 2 : NO 2

2wice

magazine of the year 1998
society of publication designers

uniform

todd oldham
annette meyer
nudie
geoffrey beene
stewardesses
richard martin
maids
karen kimmel
doormen
cadets
wonder woman
geisha
superman
mark wigley
bunny
the art guys
muzak

2wice (*US, Issues 1,3 & 4, 1997/8) 210 x 290mm*
Published twice a year – hence the name – this magazine changes its design and content to relate to a different theme each issue. A combination of a distinctive logo and precisely researched photography gives these covers a strong, consistent presence despite the relatively abstract nature of the imagery. Only the photograph used on Issue 3, 'Self', resembles a typical magazine cover, featuring a close-up shot of Dolly the cloned sheep. Editor and art director *J. Abbott Miller*

DAZED

ISSUE THIRTY-THREE

**THIRD ANNIVERSARY SPECIAL
FASHION ISSUE**

ONLY £1

INSTANT WIN SCRATCH & SEE

STARRING:
NOBUYOSHI ARAKI
NICK KNIGHT
HELENA CHRISTENSEN
DAVID LACHAPELLE
KARL LAGERFELD
GLEN LUCHFORD
RAYMOND MEIER
STEVEN MEISEL
JEAN BAPTISTE MONDINO
HELMUT NEWTON
DAVID SIMS
MARIO SORRENTI
JUERGEN TELLER
MARIO TESTINO

PHIL BICKER
ANNA COCKBURN
KATY ENGLAND
TIBOR KALMAN
CATHY KASTERINE
RICHARD PANDISCIO
NANCY ROHDE
CARINE ROITFELD
CHRISTOPH STEINEGGER
VENETIA SCOTT
LEE SWILLINGHAM
MELANIE WARD
ALEX WHITE
CAMILLE BIDAULT-
WADDINGTON

33
SCRATCH & SEE
AUG 1997 UK£1.00 US$4.95
ITEM UK€2.95 1997 ISSN 0961-9704

HELENA CHRISTENSEN PHOTOGRAPHED BY RANKIN

9 770961 970988

08

DAZED

PIONEER

THIRD ANNIVERSARY SPECIAL
FASHION ISSUE

ONLY £1

STARRING:

NOBUYOSHI ARAKI
NICK KNIGHT
HELENA CHRISTENSEN
DAVID LACHAPELLE
KARL LAGERFELD
GLEN LUCHFORD
RAYMOND MEIER
STEVEN MEISEL
JEAN BAPTISTE MONDINO
HELMUT NEWTON
DAVID SIMS
MARIO SORRENTI
JUERGEN TELLER
MARIO TESTINO

PHIL BICKER
ANNA COCKBURN
KATY ENGLAND
TIBOR KALMAN
CATHY KASTERINE
RICHARD PANDISCIO
NANCY ROHDE
CARINE ROITFELD
CHRISTOPH STEINEGGER
VENETIA SCOTT
LEE SWILLINGHAM
MELANIE WARD
ALEX WHITE
CAMILLE BIDAULT-
WADDINGTON

NO★ ★WIN

INSTANT WIN SCRATCH & SEE

33 SCRATCH & SEE
AUG 1997 UK£1.00 US$4.95
[730 LM£30 C$3.95 Y800 ISSN 0961-9704]

9 770961 970988

08

Dazed & Confused *(UK, Issue 33, August 1997) 230 x 297mm*
Best-known for its photography, this independent magazine also excels at combining sponsorship and technology to provide extras such as gatefold sections. In this case, scratchcard ink has been used to tease the reader.
Art director *Matt Roach*
Photographer *Rankin*

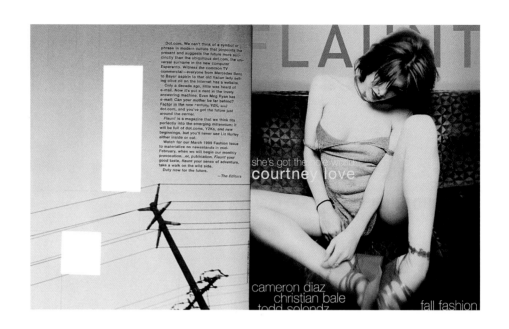

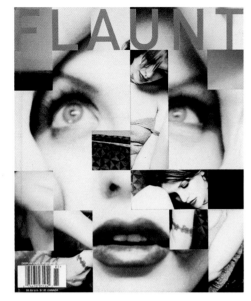

Issue 1, Autumn/Winter 1998

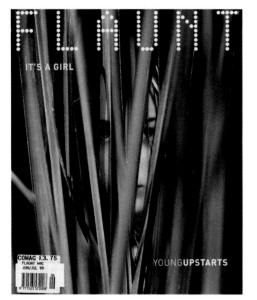

Issue 5, June/July 1999

THIS PAGE **Flaunt** *(US) 230 x 275mm*
Each issue features a double cover, the top part being die-cut so the bottom part is visible through the holes. The top example lets the creative team collage two photographs of Courtney Love; the bottom example is a more literal use of the device, making Leelee Sobieski appear to stare at the reader from behind some leaves. Both covers open to reveal the whole picture.
Art directors *Eric Roinestad and Jim Turner*

OPPOSITE **Blad** *(The Netherlands, Issue 4, 1995) 230 x 297mm*
This cover uses a similar die-cut technique to illustrate a quotation from an interview with Robert Frank. 'I'm always looking outside,' reads the black type on the cover; open the cover and the seemingly random die-cut shapes complete Frank's words, 'trying to look inside'.
Art director *Hans Wolf*

BLAD 4/95

fl. 20,- | Bfr. 400

★ I'm always looking inside.

De inhoud van Robert Frank*

+ De binnenkant van melk + De buitenkant van Fancy + Het uitzicht volgens Hofstede + Het perspectief van Milchstrasse

try ing to look in side.

©olofon

Issue 34, June 1994

Issue 49, September 1994

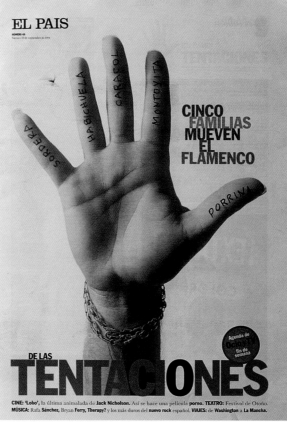

Issue 158, November 1996

Issue 160, November 1996

Tentaciones *(Spain) 295 x 410mm*

The fact that this is a free supplement to *El Pais* newspaper meant the covers were free of the normal commercial constraints such as a constant position for the title. Instead, a strong visual style was developed: the image was always cut out on a white background with the title across it at whatever height suited. One letter in the title would be picked out in a different colour ('like the apple in the Garden of Eden') to echo the title, which translates as Temptations.
Art director *Fernando Gutiérrez*

weekend

The Guardian

The world at their feet
Kathy Acker meets the Spice Girls

The Guardian Weekend *(UK, May 1997) 290 x 370mm*

As a newspaper supplement the need to sell is less insistent, but this remains a brave cover. To avoid a photo shoot with The Spice Girls resulting in the standard over-styled, carefully posed picture, the photographer was commissioned to take pictures of parts of the girls. The result was this shot in which the subjects are immediately recognizable despite the fact that only their feet and shoes are visible.

Art director *Mark Porter*
Photographer *Nigel Shafran*

Independent
Magazine

02/09/95

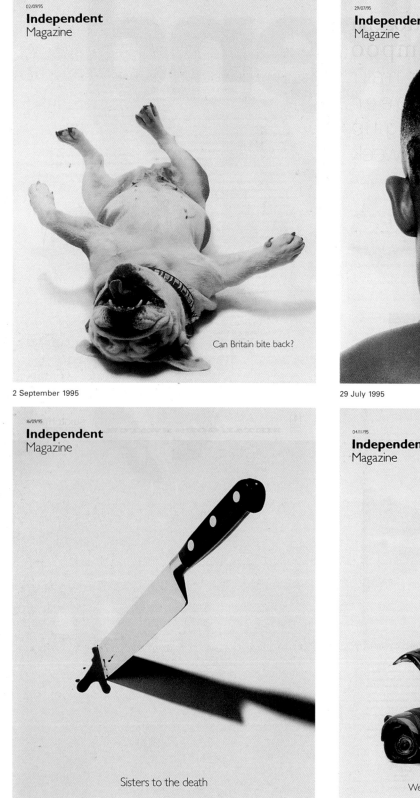

Can Britain bite back?

2 September 1995

Independent
Magazine

29/07/95

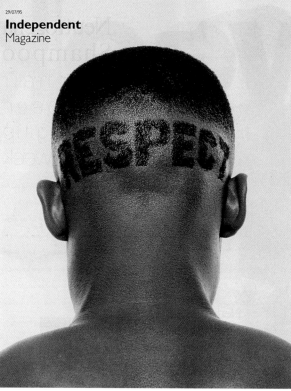

29 July 1995

Independent
Magazine

16/09/95

Sisters to the death

16 September 1995

Independent
Magazine

04/11/95

Welcome to France

4 November 1995

The Independent Magazine (UK) 280 x 355mm
These covers for a newspaper supplement demonstrate a creative solution to an awkward problem: despite having to be devised and photographed during the week preceding publication, the editor wanted to lead with conceptual features rather than the typical interview feature. The style that developed was a clever response. Able to avoid the hard sell, they nonetheless set up their own identity that uses humour and conceptual ideas to set themselves apart from other supplements. The point is intrigue rather than explanation.
Art director Vince Frost

Issue 52, February 1999, Pornography

Vanidad *(Spain)*

'So many magazines just follow the same formula now, especially youth magazines. If you're doing a magazine for young people it should have issues that are affecting them, not just Johnny Depp on the cover.'

FERNANDO GUTIÉRREZ

Noviembre 1998
425 ptas.

vanidad 50

CULTURA GAY

MARILYN MANSON
A LOS QUE AMAN
CINE IDIOTA
MUNDO VIRTUAL

00050

8 424094 037650

vanidad

TELEVISIÓN

CHRISTINA RICCI
TOKYO
CLUBBING 70'S

Fotografía: Sara Zorraquino

vanidad

DIOS

MUERTOS DE RISA
CLONACIÓN NIPONA
FROMHEADTOTOE
FANZINES

Fotografía: Jesús López

Issue 51, December 1998, Television

Issue 53, March 1999, God

Fernando Gutiérrez redesigned *Vanidad*, a Spanish style magazine, in 1998. From the masthead right through the magazine he changed its look completely. The most controversial change was the introduction of a graphic logo, an inverted capital A, to replace the traditional masthead. 'I wanted to create an icon. A is a symbolic letter, the beginning,' explains Gutiérrez, 'To see the beginning upside down makes you uneasy. It's the form of a V, for Vanidad, and also the head of a bull. It was a reaction to the rules of editorial, an attempt to break them down.' The result is a very strong but very abstract masthead.

That attempt extends right through the magazine. Showing a clear understanding of the requirements of signposting and pacing, Gutiérrez has created a versatile set of components for the magazine's designers to use, while turning most accepted rules of editorial design on their head. With the exception of the running heads (which repeat the first letter of each word of the headline) no type is larger than 18pt, the headlines running in tiny bold capitals. A ruthlessly simple colour palette – black, white and red – combines with the generous use of white space to hold the editorial apart from the advertising and make the magazine surprisingly easy to navigate.

While Johnny Depp and his fellow celebrities still feature inside the magazine, they have been replaced on the cover by images relating to the special reports the magazine compiles on issues such as drugs, porn, television and revolution. These images are chosen for their directness and are sometimes shot specially – for example the two action men getting into bed together for a cover about gay culture – or are sourced from libraries.

Gutiérrez has now handed the project over to the magazine's in-house team. He is clear about how it should move on from here: 'I don't want it to stay the same – I want it to evolve. I want them to say "OK it's springtime, let's change it". They should keep changing. Change the typefaces, the grid.'

06/99   Con los cinco sentidos

05/99   Fuego en las calles

04/99   Bésame mucho

03/99   ¡Dios mio de mi vida!

02/99   I wanna be a Porno-Star

12/98-1/99   mamá televisión

11/98   ¿Quien sabe donde?

56   55   54   53   52   51   50

Pace

'The word magazine means storage space for dynamite. A magazine is full of surprises and it can explode. It can go off at any time.'

FERNANDO GUTIÉRREZ

It is the element of surprise more than any other quality that marks a publication out as a magazine. Whatever format they appear in, magazines rely on presenting various types of information in a carefully prepared running order. In this respect they are a time-based medium, and need to be designed with that in mind. The designer and editor must consciously vary both the content itself and the method(s) of presenting the content throughout each issue to provide changes in pace and thus keep surprising the reader. This is an important issue regardless of whether the magazine in question is an international mainstream title like *Vogue*, or a small-scale independent title like *SleazeNation*.

The first manifestation of an issue of a magazine is the flatplan. Like a film storyboard this diagrammatic representation of the issue allows the editor and designer to fit together all the parts of the magazine and try different running orders. This will include advertising, the presence of which is essential to help make a magazine feel like a magazine. It is partly to accommodate advertising that the most common overall structure is to sandwich longer features (the 'well') between a series of shorter articles at the front and the back. These shorter articles soak up all the ads, leaving the central well clear, or relatively clear, of advertising. Fashion magazines such as *Vogue* and *Harper's Bazaar* announce the start of the well with a page summing up the fashion themes that follow. Issue 6 of *Self Service* (France) is divided into these three sections and gives each one its technical title: Front, Well, Back. Such sections may have their own dedicated design rules –

variations in column width and typeface – to help define their differences.

But however carefully this running order is compiled, the reader is at liberty to enter the magazine at any point and to navigate freely in any direction. Some readers will start by dipping into the middle of a magazine, others will turn straight to a favourite regular feature. Some will glance casually through the contents page, some will turn straight to the cover story that attracted them to buy the magazine in the first place. Having read the first piece they will then read on, or restart at the contents page, or have another flick through to see what catches their eye. The magazine may be tossed to one side while a phone call is taken, forgotten about and only picked up again days later. There is no single way through a magazine, which makes the role of the designer that much tougher, as at the heart of their job is the requirement to help the reader find their way around, to signpost the content.

While historically magazines have ignored this liberty of movement and continued to present their pages as a single series of carefully delineated features, today's computer programs have enabled designers to acknowledge the freedom readers have. The front section of *Wired* (US), 'Electric Word', is typical of such a section in most ways but has a strand of mini-stories that run through the middle of each page, jumping mid-sentence from page to page. In an issue devoted entirely to a single architectural project, *Architecture New York* (US) ran the various interviews and essays alongside each other, the stories in this case jumping from page to page across up to nine pages. While serving as an

interesting device, this also had the advantage of permitting the available photographic material to be spread across the whole issue rather than just be placed with the single relevant interview.

Similarly, in a ten-page feature about Benetton art director Oliviero Toscani, *Eye* (UK) ran four commentaries on his work alongside each other; readers had to travel from the first page through the feature four times before completing the article. In a further break with convention, the whole article was turned on its side. As art director Nick Bell explains, 'We turned the article on its side in order to recontextualize the Toscani billboard ads by running them as full-page images, as if they were ads in our magazine.'

Asked to design a special edition about computers for *Die Zeit* magazine (Germany), art directors Johannes Essl and Oliver Kartak of Austrian company DMC decided to separate the words and pictures. This could easily have destroyed any sense of pace and rendered both pictures and words unapproachable. In fact it works very well. The first 19 pages contain 33 numbered pictures. Each one relates to a numbered written piece in the back half of the issue. These texts run in numerical order, while the pictures are presented out of numerical order, allowing the designers to develop a purely visual essay. All advertising is confined to the back section and serves to lighten what would otherwise have been heavy, text-laden pages.

Apart (Germany) adopted similarly ruthless devices. This youth culture magazine grew from a college fanzine. Art director Mike Meiré spent the first six issues learning about magazines, altering everything with each issue. 'After those issues I

Pace

was bored with all the possibilities; I decided to give up doing decoration and cut to corporate design, to a strong, sharp identity.' A set of very strict rules was introduced. The only font was Futura, and each issue featured a different but very tightly defined grid. 'I enjoyed the process of setting up a system and making the material work to it. We were deliberately walking the edge between boring and interesting.'

All this experimentation increases the need for good signposting. The focal point for signposting is the contents page. This will usually appear as the first editorial page and list everything the magazine contains along with page number references. There are certain assumptions made here: not least that page numbers run in numerical order from the front cover. Issue two of *Speak* (US) played with this convention, altering it but creating its own logic by making the centre spread of the magazine the contents page and numbering it as page 00. The pages preceding the contents run as minus numbers, those after the contents as plus numbers. Had it been numbered the front cover would have been page -45.

The presence of a contents page presupposes that each page is numbered; this is signposting at its most basic. In fact everything on the page is a form of signpost. Each magazine creates its own look and rules to help the reader build a relationship with it and to create familiarity.

More than any other magazine in the fashion market British *Vogue* needs to work hard to distinguish its editorial from the increasingly sophisticated advertisements. To do so art director Robin Derrick has established a very simple set of typographic rules, his 'design fascism'. Each issue Derrick selects a form of Gill Sans that will be used for the headlines, giving a very strong identity to each magazine. Gill has become so identified with the magazine that when he recently began a re-design he was unable to decide on an alternative font. Instead he commissioned a new mono-line version of the entire Gill family, adding two new weights. This simple device allows him to maintain a basic consistency issue by issue while varying each specific one.

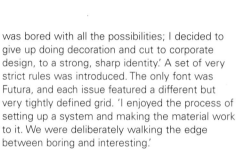

Self Service (France, Issue 6, *Autumn/Winter 1997*) *230 x 300mm*
For this issue, the three main sections of this fashion magazine – the front, the well and the back – were labelled with full-page announcements.
Art direction *Work In Progress*

TOP **Speak** (US, Issue 2, 1996) 254 x 305mm
This contents list plays with convention in a number of ways. Not only is it essentially unclear, consisting of small type reversed out of a complex image, but it also appears as the centre spread of the magazine. As a result, all pages preceding it have minus page numbers.
Art director *David Carson*

BOTTOM **Econy** (Germany, April/May 1999)
This contents page gives simple, direct information, using photographs to sell 12 main features.
Art director *Mike Meiré*

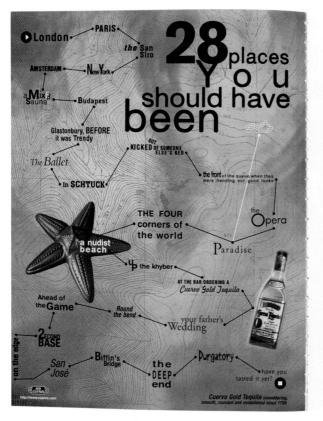

TOP **Dazed & Confused** (UK, Issue 38, 1998) 230 x 298mm
Unrelenting type gives character to this simple, clear contents page
Art director *Darren Ellis*

BOTTOM **Big** (Spain, Issue 7) 295 x 410mm
Contents page using page numbers as graphic decoration.
Creative director *Vince Frost*

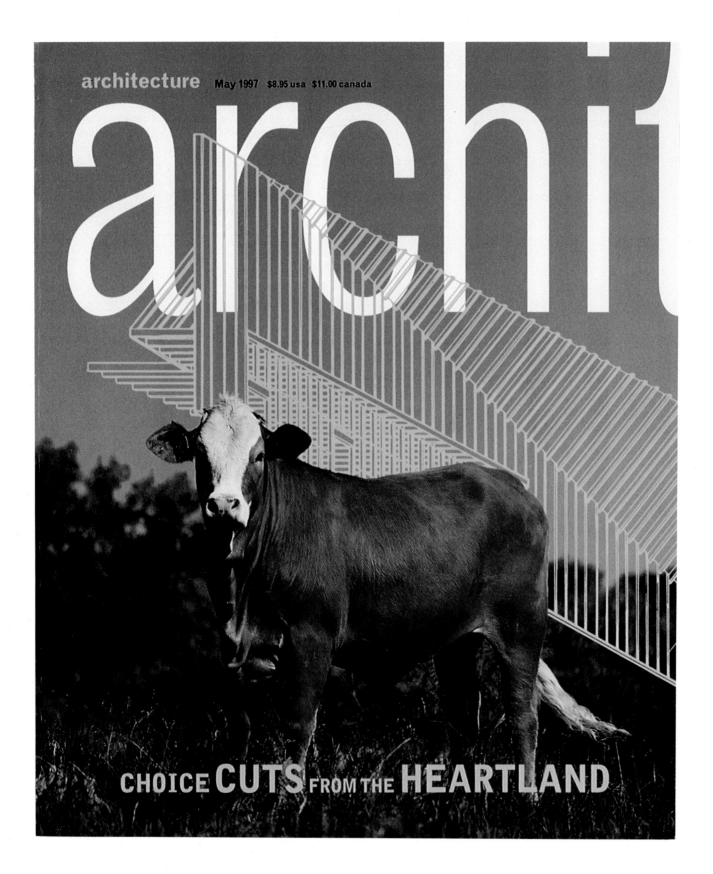

architecture May 1997 $8.95 usa $11.00 canada

archi

CHOICE **CUTS** FROM THE **HEARTLAND**

tecture

DESIGN

Architecture
(US, 1997) 230 x 275mm
The logo runs off the cover on to the contents spread, reflecting how the scale of a building is often beyond our perceptual range. A happy by-product is the way the split word draws the reader from the cover into the contents list.
Art directors *J. Abbott Miller and Luke Hayman*

PHOTOS STEPHANE SEDNAOUI

L'incendiaire

*Shirley Manson affirme qu'elle n'est pas, a priori,
le genre de fille qui réussit. Faut croire qu'elle
a eu chaud : à peine débarrassée de son surnom
"œil de grenouille", elle a failli chanter les clowns
tristes dans un groupe au nom scato...
Puis Garbage est arrivé et a mis le feu aux poudres.*

"Je me demande bien ce que fabrique mon coiffeur...", s'interroge Shirley Manson avec sa voix de gamine malicieuse. C'est qu'il est très tôt. L'heure où les musiciens rentrent de leur virée nocturne pour aller s'affaler dans leur chambre d'hôtel. Mais malgré sa réputation de fêtarde déjantée, Shirley est déjà au boulot : en pleine métamorphose, elle se prépare pour une émission de télé. Lascive à souhait, dans le rôle de la bombe sexuelle du rock'n'roll, elle porte un peignoir blanc, un string Calvin Klein et deux anneaux d'argent au pied.

Avec son franc-parler, la chanteuse écossaise a surpris plus d'un journaliste par ses confessions érotiques. Si l'on en juge par les textes de ses chansons et par son image médiatique, c'est une femme dominatrice et espiègle, obsédée par le sexe et les jeux de l'esprit, qui se moque bien de ce qu'on pense d'elle.

Garbage était réuni à New York dans le cadre de leur tournée américaine, avec Alanis Morissette. Et c'est ici que se sont achevés leurs dix-huit mois de tribulations pour la promotion de leur deuxième album, *Version 2.0*. Les musiciens ont ainsi écumé six villes, où ils ont enchaîné plusieurs concerts et le tournage du clip de *You Look so Fine* (qui sort en Europe le 24 mai). Dans le clip, réalisé par Stéphane Sednaoui, on voit une Shirley en plein délire romantique, séduisant le trop beau surfer Kelly Slater. Avec une pointe d'ironie, la chanteuse décrit cet épisode comme "un petit Bergman, très sensuel, très beau, et très symbolique".

Shirley Manson, trente-deux ans, quoique ravie d'avoir pu échapper quelques mois à la vie provinciale de Madison (Wisconsin), où le groupe a élu domicile, commence à accuser la fatigue des voyages. La tournée a démarré peu de temps après son mariage avec Eddie Farrel, sculpteur et marionnettiste écossais qui reste bien sagement au pays (Queensferry) tandis que sa femme part sur les routes. Comment Shirley s'accomode-t-elle de cette séparation forcée, elle qui n'a jamais cessé de clamer sur tous les toits qu'elle s'était lancée dans le rock'n'roll uniquement pour le sexe ?

"C'est une sorte de célibat forcé, déclare-t-elle de sa voix sifflante d'asthmatique, qui a ses propres plaisirs pervers." Elle rit en évoquant l'idée qu'elle et son mari ont recours à des petits jeux masturbatoires à la Anaïs Nin. "C'est tout nous, ça, glousse-t-elle. Toujours dans des chambres séparées ! Je sais, ça peut paraître étrange.

24

Haut et jupe en tulle
brodé, MANOLO (sur commande).
Chaussures, SONIA RYKIEL.

Numéro *(France, Issue 4, June 1999) 232 x 300mm*
One of a number of publications concentrating on the
image above type, this fashion magazine picks out the
page numbers as the boldest element of the page design.
Art director *Thomas Lenthal*
Photographer *Stéphane Sednaoui*

Top en mousseline bordeaux
et jupe en superpositions
de mousselines jaune et blanche,
MASAKI MATSUSHIMA. Escarpins
à paillettes, SONIA RYKIEL.

mais je vous assure que c'est très bien. Moi, je tourne depuis l'âge de quinze ans, et quand j'ai rencontré mon mari, j'étais pas mal en tournée, je partais des mois entiers, ce qui fait qu'on a une grande expérience dans ce domaine. C'est un être exceptionnel, un très grand communicateur, et c'est pour ça que ça fonctionne. C'est uniquement grâce à lui. C'est un saint."

Les médias l'ont souvent accusée d'être une carriériste au sang froid. J'attire alors son attention sur le fait que cette longue séparation conjugale ne fait rien pour arranger sa réputation. "Je ne me laisse pas émouvoir par les balivernes qui sont colportées sur moi dans la presse, répond-elle. Mais je pense que mes proches doivent bien se marrer en lisant que je suis une opportuniste sans cœur. Tout dans ma vie suggère le contraire. Je ne me suis jamais fait de plan de carrière. Tout s'est fait un peu par hasard et de façon très décontractée. Bien sûr, comme ça marche bien, les gens sont méfiants. Je ne suis pas le genre de fille qui réussit, a priori."

Lorsqu'on passe quelques instants avec la séduisante chanteuse, on constate en effet qu'elle est plutôt modeste. On a beaucoup écrit

27

"Je ne me suis jamais fait de plan
de carrière. Tout s'est fait un peu par hasard
et de façon très décontractée."

sur Shirley Manson, le vilain petit canard, qui estime que sa tignasse rousse est plutôt un handicap dans une course à la réussite où toutes les autres concurrentes sont blondes. "Des cheveux roux comme ça, c'était vraiment un mauvais départ dans la vie, dit-elle. Du moins, c'est ce que je pensais quand j'étais gamine. Surtout venant d'un petit pays comme l'Ecosse, dans les années 70-80, où c'était la misère, le chômage. C'est sûr que ça ne m'a pas vraiment aidée. J'étais dans un groupe qui n'avait aucun projet, j'avais des rapports difficiles avec les médias et, en plus de ça, je n'écrivais pas encore mes chansons. Me voir propulsée musicienne et leader d'un groupe de rock, ça m'a fait tout drôle."

Shirley Manson est née à Edimbourg, en Ecosse, d'un père professeur d'université et d'une mère chanteuse amateur. Bien qu'assez extravertie et plutôt créative, elle était consciente de son physique peu commun (les autres gosses l'appelaient "œil de grenouille") et de son drôle d'accent distingué. Comme il se doit, cette incarnation de la révolte adolescente a elle-même passé quelques années difficiles. "J'étais têtue, et sans cesse en rupture avec mes parents. Un vrai cauchemar, mais j'avais la pêche. J'ai toujours eu une énergie phénoménale. Je ne sais pas du tout d'où ça me vient. Je suis plutôt du genre révolté, et c'est ça qui me fait avancer."

En 1995, après plusieurs faux départs dans le monde du spectacle, et trois années humiliantes passées derrière un comptoir de grand magasin, Shirley Manson est contactée par un groupe américain formé par Vig (producteur de Nirvana, des Smashing Pumpkins et de Nine Inch Nails), Steve Marker et Duke Erikson. Les trois musiciens avaient vu Shirley sur MTV dans la vidéo Suffocate Me, qu'elle avait tournée pour son groupe d'alors, Angelfish, et ils avaient fini par

retrouver sa trace. Au moment où Shirley est arrivée parmi eux, ils en étaient encore à se chercher un nom. Ils avaient vaguement pensé à Rectal Drip (incontinence rectale), et envisageaient de sortir un album intitulé Sad Alcoholic Clowns (tristes clowns alcooliques).

"Je n'aurais pas pu vendre ça de façon convaincante, commente Shirley. Moi, j'ai plutôt le vin gai, et je ne suis pas du genre agressif. C'est parce que j'évacue tout au quotidien. Je fais tout péter. Je ne nourris jamais de mauvaises pensées."

Spécialiste des formules chocs ("Je coûte cher à l'entretien, comme toutes les filles intelligentes"), Shirley Manson est franche du collier et ne rentre pas volontiers dans les clichés auxquels beaucoup de stars se laissent aller à l'occasion d'une interview. A la différence de nombre de ses contemporains, elle ne se sent pas obligée de saupoudrer ses déclarations de quelques propos choisis sur l'action humanitaire, sur la sauvegarde des bébés phoques, sur son enfance difficile, que sais-je encore...

"Je pense que pas mal de gens célèbres et de musiciens ont trop tendance à survaluer leur rapport aux médias, dit-elle. Ils finissent par avoir peur de ce qu'ils vont dire et, du coup, tout est préparé à l'avance avec un conseiller en communication. Moi, je ne suis pas prête à vivre comme ça, à sacrifier ma joie de vivre à mon image."

"Même quand on croit qu'on donne
la meilleure image de soi, il y a quelqu'un
pour la détourner de façon négative."

28

Elle fait remarquer au passage que même quelqu'un comme Madonna, qui est littéralement obsédée par son image, peut être totalement mal interprétée et mal comprise. Depuis qu'elle est sous le feu des projecteurs, Shirley Manson a appris à lâcher prise. "Même quand on croit qu'on donne la meilleure image de soi, il y a toujours quelqu'un pour la détourner de façon négative. Alors il faut se dire qu'on n'en a rien à foutre, même si quelque part entre Brighton et Lyon, il y a quelqu'un que ne vous connaît pas et qui pense a priori du mal de vous. Bien sûr, il arrive que les médias essaient de s'immiscer dans votre vie privée, de vous faire parler de votre famille ou de vos relations avec vos amis, et là, ça peut faire mal. Mais, en général, s'ils racontent des mensonges, je m'en moque."

Shirley Manson s'intéresse davantage à l'envers du décor, à ce qu'on ne montre pas, même si c'est sordide. "Ce qui me fascine vraiment, c'est le 'sexual politics', dit-elle. Mais je ne suis pas seulement obsédée par le sexe et la dépravation. Je m'intéresse aux autres, pas seulement à moi. En regardant autour de moi, je me rends compte que les gens ne sont pas toujours très honnêtes sur eux-mêmes, qu'ils ont peur de ce qu'ils ressentent, de ce qu'ils ont envie de dire, et qu'ils ne savent pas toujours très bien comment le dire. Moi, ce qui m'intéresse le plus, c'est ce que les gens essaient de cacher, pas ce qu'ils veulent montrer à tout prix."

Horacio Silva

En juillet, Garbage poursuit sa tournée européenne (concert le 24 à Vannes).

Veste sans manches et jupe
portefeuille, OLIVIER THEYSKENS.
Réalisation : Havana Laffitte.
Maquillage : Gina Monachi pour
Bianca Blythe Beauty.
Coiffure : Kevin Ryan pour
Sebastian chez Beauty & Photo.

Amizkal

¿Qué es Iberia aparte de un tinte con colores antiguos o unos aviones con un logotipo feo? ¿Iberia es un trozo de tierra?, ¿es una idea de alguien que vivió, que vive en una casi isla?, ¿con montañas atravesadas de arriba abajo?, ¿barrancos que llevan ríos secos o acequias desbordantes de agua cuando llueve? Cuando hace mucho tiempo, mucho o muchísimo. Uno ve el mapa y tenía forma y estaba centrada, aislada. Uno va caminando por Iberia y hay mucha montaña sí, pero sobre todo hay mucha loma, montaña repelada por el viento y por el tiempo.

Iberia es vieja, antigua, amarrón desde arriba, tiene cielos grandes con nubes que vienen desde el Atlántico. Y brisas del lago Mediterráneo. Tanta playa para arremojarse los pies. Olas pequeñas, suaves tontorronas por una parte y olas grandes, bestiales, que hacen ruidos de aplauso en las playas con piedras. El Atlántico es un mar grande que trae un sabor americano a las playas de Portugal. El Cantábrico, que es un mar muy suyo, cerrado en sí mismo, parece un océano y es un lago cabreado. El mar del estrecho, el de Gibraltar, es un río amazónico que tiene prisa por ser atlántico.

Y desde Tarifa se ven las montañas de Tetuán o de África del Rif con barcas de pateros que vienen y no van. Arriba, arriba del todo como una presa, una montaña frontera que te gusta la nieve, los Pirineos. Siempre dicen,

Geografía física

hasta aquí. Pero siempre por la derecha se les cuela un trozo de Provenza, Languedoc, un pedazo de Europa verde, de norte con pinos y casas de piedra, le llaman Catalunya. Iberia huele a fenicios con barcos llenos de monedas y cosas metálicas de fundición. Iberia es mucho más Iberia en verano. Con las higueras alimentando moscas pegajosas y cabras buscando su sombra. Iberia sabe a romero y esparto. Iberia con mucha playa en el litoral y al interior un mar inmenso, un mar de terrones, piedrones y pocos árboles.

Iberia diríamos es un país. Pero cada vez que coges un camino, una carretera, a las dos o tres curvas estás en otro país. Iberia es todo eso pues el mar y las montañas lo separan de lo otro y lo suyo, es una Galicia que no quiere ser Portugal, un Alentejo que da la espalda a su Extremadura, un Toledo esperando un aeropuerto para despegar otra vez. Y cuando llegas arriba entras por una esquina a un valle verde, el País Vasco, con casas de pisos perdidas por las montañetas. Y abajo Cádiz, tierra de flamencos y patos blancos que comen pipas con sal. No sé, quizás Iberia es como un continente a varios a la vez, concentrados. Hay de todo y todo es tan diferente y todo es tan igual. Total cuatro casas agrupadas de vez en cuando y es medio bancales con olivos, uva, pinos y alguna paloma torcaz, señores y mños y mñas, abuelas que hablan como en la tele, o como los abuelos un día les contaban cuentos. Si,

El arma de –

un crimen

Matador (Spain, Issue C, 1997) 300 x 400mm
Published once a year, this independent magazine combines photography and literature based on a theme, in this case 'A New Spain'. Each issue is designed to a different but strict grid and uses just one typeface. The pages shown are in numerical but not always consecutive order; they demonstrate how even a very simple design can be varied to alter the pace of a magazine. Starting from the top left, working right and down: a double page spread of text; text opposite left-hand picture; text opposite right-hand picture; text opposite left-hand picture again; three spreads of pictures; two spreads of text; as this system starts to repeat, a different style of page – larger type on a colour background; and finally text with large headline.
Art director *Fernando Gutiérrez*

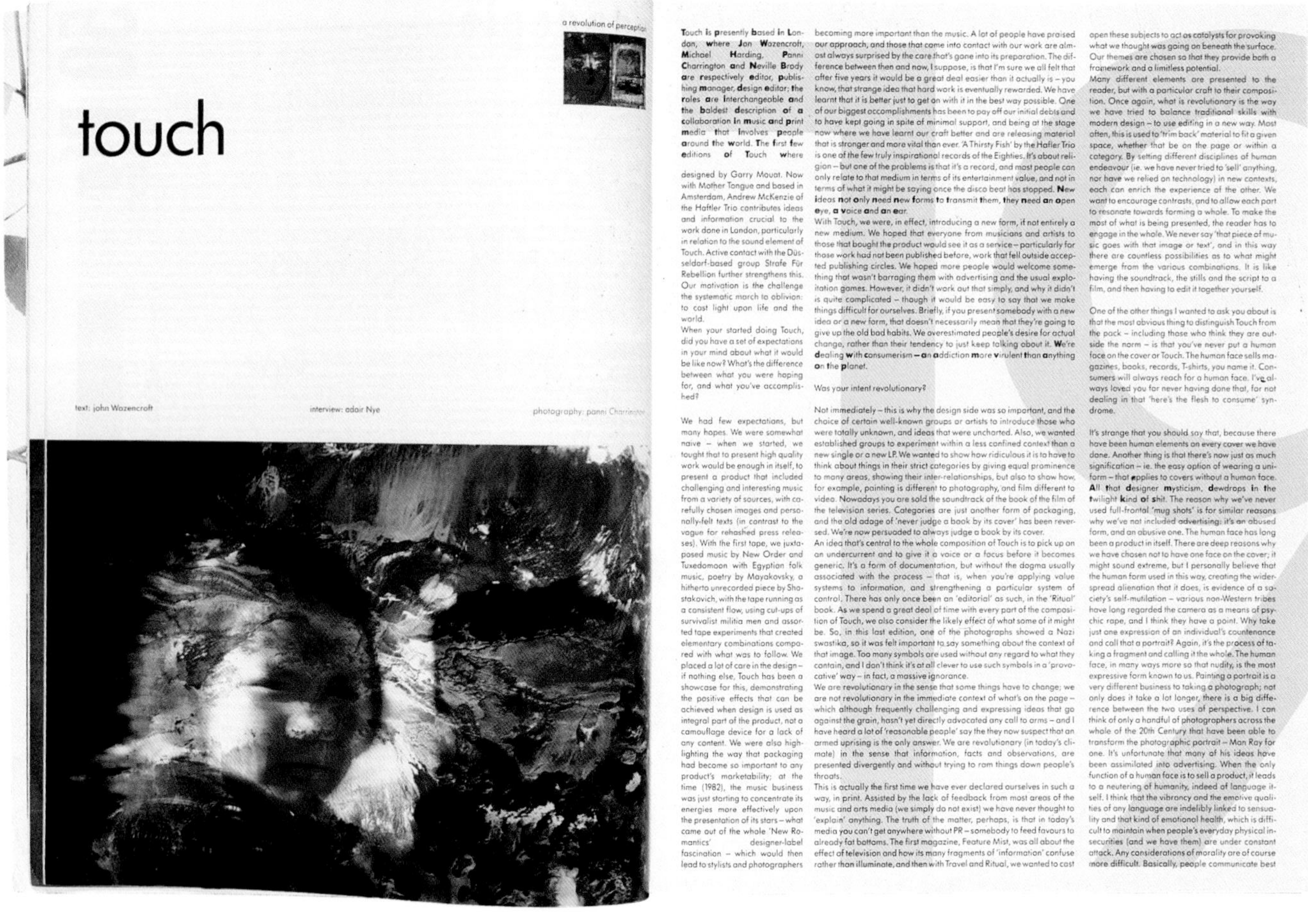

a revolution of perception

touch

text: john Wazencroft interview: adair Nye photography: panni Charrington

Touch is presently based in London, where Jon Wazencroft, Michael Harding, Panni Charrington and Neville Brody are respectively editor, publishing manager, design editor; the roles are Interchangeable and the baldest description of a collaboration in music and print media that Involves people around the world. The first few editions of Touch where

designed by Garry Mouat. Now with Mother Tongue and based in Amsterdam, Andrew McKenzie of the Haftler Trio contributes ideas and information crucial to the work done in London, particularly in relation to the sound element of Touch. Active contact with the Düsseldorf-based group Strafe Für Rebellion further strengthens this. Our motivation is the challenge the systematic march to oblivion: to cast light upon life and the world.

When your started doing Touch, did you have a set of expectations in your mind about what it would be like now? What's the difference between what you were hoping for, and what you've accomplished?

We had few expectations, but many hopes. We were somewhat naive – when we started, we tought that to present high quality work would be enough in itself, to present a product that included challenging and interesting music from a variety of sources, with carefully chosen images and personally-felt texts (in contrast to the vogue for rehashed press releases). With the first tape, we juxtaposed music by New Order and Tuxedomoon with Egyptian folk music, poetry by Mayakovsky, a hitherto unrecorded piece by Shostakovich, with the tape running as a consistent flow, using cut-ups of survivalist militia men and assorted tape experiments that created elementary combinations compared with what was to follow. We placed a lot of care in the design – if nothing else, Touch has been a showcase for this, demonstrating the positive effects that can be achieved when design is used as integral part of the product, not a camouflage device for a lack of any content. We were also highlighting the way that packaging had become so important to any product's marketability; at the time (1982), the music business was just starting to concentrate its energies more effectively upon the presentation of its stars – what came out of the whole 'New Romantics' designer-label fascination – which would then lead to stylists and photographers becoming more important than the music. A lot of people have praised our approach, and those that come into contact with our work are almost always surprised by the care that's gone into its preparation. The difference between then and now, I suppose, is that I'm sure we all felt that after five years it would be a great deal easier than it actually is – you know, that strange idea that hard work is eventually rewarded. We have learnt that it is better just to get on with it in the best way possible. One of our biggest accomplishments has been to pay off our initial debts and to have kept going in spite of minimal support, and being at the stage now where we have learnt our craft better and are releasing material that is stronger and more vital than ever. 'A Thirsty Fish' by the Hafler Trio is one of the few truly inspirational records of the Eighties. It's about religion – but one of the problems is that it's a record, and most people can only relate to that medium in terms of its entertainment value, and not in terms of what it might be saying once the disco beat has stopped. **New ideas not only need new forms to transmit them, they need an open eye, a voice and an ear.**

With Touch, we were, in effect, introducing a new form, if not entirely a new medium. We hoped that everyone from musicians and artists to those that bought the product would see it as a service – particularly for those work had not been published before, work that fell outside accepted publishing circles. We hoped more people would welcome something that wasn't barraging them with advertising and the usual exploitation games. However, it didn't work out that simply, and why it didn't is quite complicated – though it would be easy to say that we make things difficult for ourselves. Briefly, if you present somebody with a new idea or a new form, that doesn't necessarily mean that they're going to give up the old bad habits. We overestimated people's desire for actual change, rather than their tendency to just keep talking about it. **We're dealing with consumerism – an addiction more virulent than anything on the planet.**

Was your intent revolutionary?

Not immediately – this is why the design side was so important, and the choice of certain well-known groups or artists to introduce those who were totally unknown, and ideas that were uncharted. Also, we wanted established groups to experiment within a less confined context than a new single or a new LP. We wanted to show how ridiculous it is to have to think about things in their strict categories by giving equal prominence to many areas, showing their inter-relationships, but also to show how, for example, painting is different to photography, and film different to video. Nowadays you are sold the soundtrack of the book of the film of the television series. Categories are just another form of packaging, and the old adage of 'never judge a book by its cover' has been reversed. We're now persuaded to always judge a book by its cover.

An idea that's central to the whole composition of Touch is to pick up on an undercurrent and to give it a voice or a focus before it becomes generic. It's a form of documentation, but without the dogma usually associated with the process – that is, when you're applying value systems to information, and strengthening a particular system of control. There has only once been an 'editorial' as such, in the 'Ritual' book. As we spend a great deal of time with every part of the composition of Touch, we also consider the likely effect of what some of it might be. So, in this last edition, one of the photographs showed a Nazi swastika, so it was felt important to say something about the context of that image. Too many symbols are used without any regard to what they contain, and I don't think it's at all clever to use such symbols in a 'provocative' way – in fact, a massive ignorance.

We are revolutionary in the sense that some things have to change; we are not revolutionary in the immediate context of what's on the page – which although frequently challenging and expressing ideas that go against the grain, hasn't yet directly advocated any call to arms – and I have heard a lot of 'reasonable people' say the they now suspect that an armed uprising is the only answer. We are revolutionary (in today's climate) in the sense that information, facts and observations, are presented divergently and without trying to ram things down people's throats.

This is actually the first time we have ever declared ourselves in such a way, in print. Assisted by the lack of feedback from most areas of the music and arts media (we simply do not exist) we have never thought to 'explain' anything. The truth of the matter, perhaps, is that in today's media you can't get anywhere without PR – somebody to feed favours to already fat bottoms. The first magazine, Feature Mist, was all about the effect of television and how its many fragments of 'information' confuse rather than illuminate, and then with Travel and Ritual, we wanted to cast open these subjects to act as catalysts for provoking what we thought was going on beneath the surface. Our themes are chosen so that they provide both a framework and a limitless potential.

Many different elements are presented to the reader, but with a particular craft to their composition. Once again, what is revolutionary is the way we have tried to balance traditional skills with modern design – to use editing in a new way. Most often, this is used to 'trim back' material to fit a given space, whether that be on the page or within a category. By setting different disciplines of human endeavour (ie. we have never tried to 'sell' anything, nor have we relied on technology) in new contexts, each can enrich the experience of the other. We want to encourage contrasts, and to allow each part to resonate towards forming a whole. To make the most of what is being presented, the reader has to engage in the whole. We never say 'that piece of music goes with that image or text', and in this way there are countless possibilities as to what might emerge from the various combinations. It is like having the soundtrack, the stills and the script to a film, and then having to edit it together yourself.

One of the other things I wanted to ask you about is that the most obvious thing to distinguish Touch from the pack – including those who think they are outside the norm – is that you've never put a human face on the cover or Touch. The human face sells magazines, books, records, T-shirts, you name it. Consumers will always reach for a human face. I've always loved you for never having done that, for not dealing in that 'here's the flesh to consume' syndrome.

It's strange that you should say that, because there have been human elements on every cover we have done. Another thing is that there's now just as much signification – ie. the easy option of wearing a uniform – that applies to covers without a human face. **All that designer mysticism, dewdrops in the twilight kind of shit.** The reason why we've never used full-frontal 'mug shots' is for similar reasons why we've not included advertising: it's an abused form, and an abusive one. The human face has long been a product in itself. There are deep reasons why we have chosen not to have one face on the cover; it might sound extreme, but I personally believe that the human form used in this way, creating the wider-spread alienation that it does, is evidence of a society's self-mutilation – various non-Western tribes have long regarded the camera as a means of psychic rape, and I think they have a point. Why take just one expression of an individual's countenance and call that a portrait? Again, it's the process of taking a fragment and calling it the whole. The human face, in many ways more so that nudity, is the most expressive form known to us. Painting a portrait is a very different business to taking a photograph; not only does it take a lot longer, there is a big difference between the two uses of perspective. I can think of only a handful of photographers across the whole of the 20th Century that have been able to transform the photographic portrait – Man Ray for one. It's unfortunate that many of his ideas have been assimilated into advertising. When the only function of a human face is to sell a product, it leads to a neutering of humanity, indeed of language itself. I think that the vibrancy and the emotive qualities of any language are indelibly linked to sensuality and that kind of emotional health, which is difficult to maintain when people's everyday physical insecurities (and we have them) are under constant attack. Any considerations of morality are of course more difficult. Basically, people communicate best

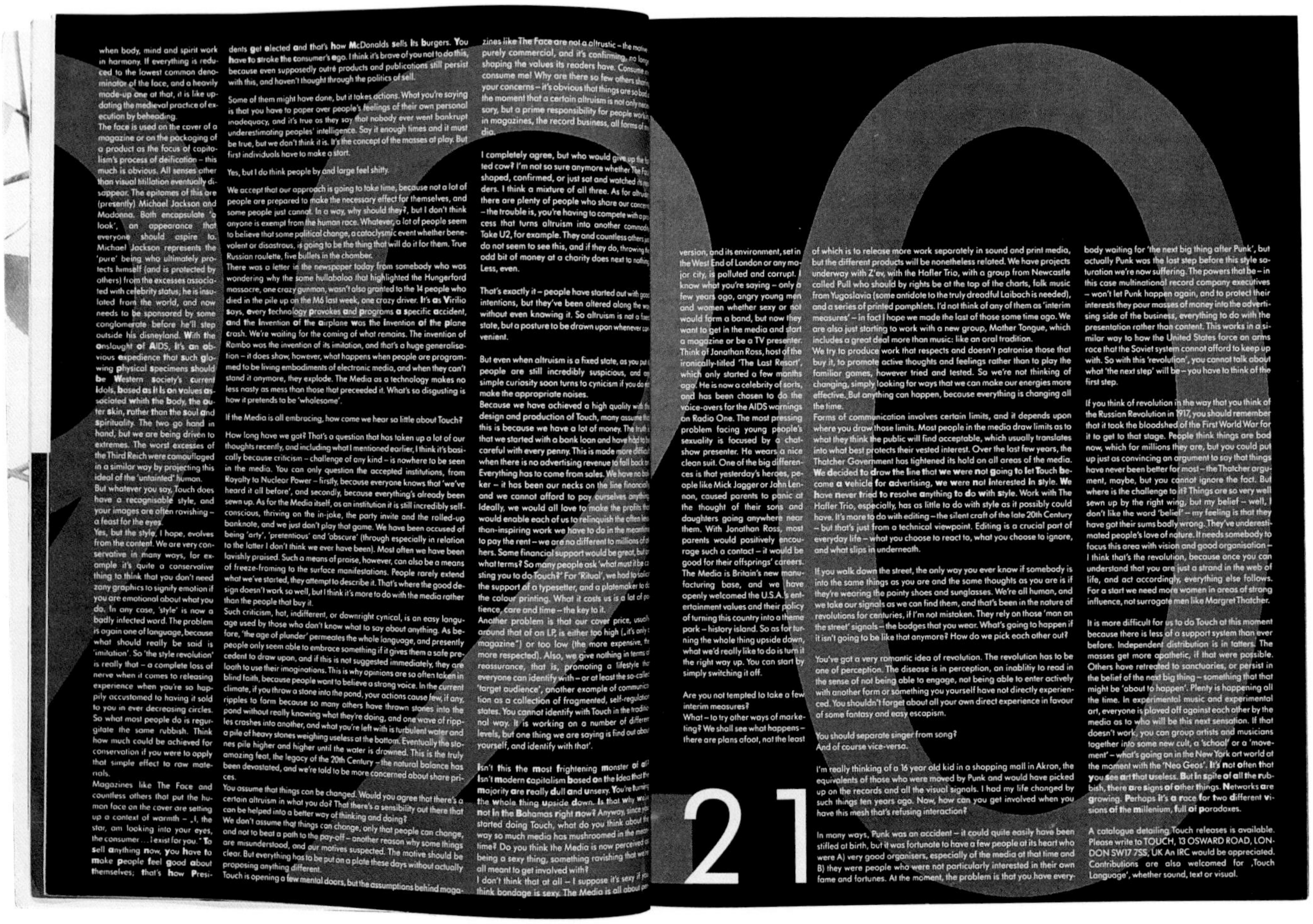

when body, mind and spirit work in harmony. If everything is reduced to the lowest common denominator of the face, and a heavily made-up one at that, it is like updating the medieval practice of execution by beheading.

The face is used on the cover of a magazine or on the packaging of a product as the focus of capitalism's process of deification – this much is obvious. All senses other than visual titillation eventually disappear. The epitomes of this are (presently) Michael Jackson and Madonna. Both encapsulate 'a look', an appearance that everyone should aspire to. Michael Jackson represents the 'pure' being who ultimately protects himself (and is protected by others) from the excesses associated with celebrity status; he is insulated from the world, and now needs to be sponsored by some conglomerate before he'll step outside his disneyland. **With the onslaught of AIDS, it's an obvious expedience that such glowing physical specimens should be Western society's current Idols, based as it is on values associated whith the body, the outer skin, rather than the soul and spirituality.** The two go hand in hand, but we are being driven to extremes. The worst excesses of the Third Reich were camouflaged in a similar way by projecting this ideal of the 'untainted' human.

But whatever you say, Touch does have a recognisable style, and your images are often ravishing – a feast for the eyes.

Yes, but the style, I hope, evolves from the content. We are very conservative in many ways, for example it's quite a conservative thing to think that you don't need zany graphics to signify emotion if you are emotional about what you do. In any case, 'style' is now a badly infected word. The problem is again one of language, because what should really be said is 'imitation'. So 'the style revolution' is really that – a complete loss of nerve when it comes to releasing experience when you're so happily accustomed to having it sold to you in ever decreasing circles. So what most people do is regurgitate the same rubbish. Think how much could be achieved for conservation if you were to apply that simple effect to raw materials.

Magazines like The Face and countless others that put the human face on the cover are setting up a context of warmth – „I, the star, am looking into your eyes, the consumer . . . I exist for you." **To sell anything now, you have to make people feel good about themselves; that's how Presidents get elected and that's how McDonalds sells its burgers. You have to stroke the consumer's ego.** I think it's brave of you not to do this, because even supposedly outré products and publications still persist with this, and haven't thought through the politics of sell.

Some of them might have done, but it takes actions. What you're saying is that you have to paper over people's feelings of their own personal inadequacy, and it's true as they say that nobody ever went bankrupt underestimating peoples' intelligence. Say it enough times and it must be true, but we don't think it is. It's the concept of the masses at play. But first individuals have to make a start.

Yes, but I do think people by and large feel shitty.

We accept that our approach is going to take time, because not a lot of people are prepared to make the necessary effect for themselves, and some people just cannot. In a way, why should they?, but I don't think anyone is exempt from the human race. Whatever, a lot of people seem to believe that some political change, a cataclysmic event whether benevolent or disastrous, is going to be the thing that will do it for them. True Russian roulette, five bullets in the chamber.

There was a letter in the newspaper today from somebody who was wondering why the same hullabaloo that highlighted the Hungerford massacre, one crazy gunman, wasn't also granted to the 14 people who died in the pile up on the M6 last week, one crazy driver. **It's as Virilio says, every technology provokes and programs a specific accident, and the Invention of the airplane was the Invention of the plane crash.** We're waiting for the coming of what remains. The invention of Rambo was the invention of its imitation, and that's a huge generalisation – it does show, however, what happens when people are programmed to be living embodiments of electronic media, and when they can't stand it anymore, they explode. The Media as a technology makes no less nasty as mess than those that preceeded it. What's so disgusting is how it pretends to be 'wholesome'.

If the Media is all embracing, how come we hear so little about Touch?

How long have we got? That's a question that has taken up a lot of our thoughts recently, and including what I mentioned earlier, I think it's basically because criticism – challenge of any kind – is nowhere to be seen in the media. You can only question the accepted institutions, from Royalty to Nuclear Power – firstly, because everyone knows that 'we've heard it all before', and secondly, because everything's already been sewn up. As for the Media itself, as an institution it is still incredibly self-conscious, thriving on the in-joke, the party invite and the rolled-up banknote, and we just don't play that game. We have been accused of being 'arty', 'pretentious' and 'obscure' (through especially in relation to the latter I don't think we ever have been). Most often we have been lavishly praised. Such a means of praise, however, can also be a means of freeze-framing to the surface manifestations. People rarely extend what we've started, they attempt to describe it. That's where the good design doesn't work so well, but I think it's more to do with the media rather than the people that buy it.

Such criticism, hot, indifferent, or downright cynical, is an easy language used by those who don't know what to say about anything. As before, 'the age of plunder' permeates the whole language, and presently people only seem able to embrace something if it gives them a safe precedent to draw upon, and if this is not suggested immediately, they are loath to use their imaginations. This is why opinions are so often taken in blind faith, because people want to believe a strong voice. In the current climate, if you throw a stone into the pond, your actions cause few, if any, ripples to form because so many others have thrown stones into the pond without really knowing what they're doing, and one wave of ripples crashes into another, and what you're left with is turbulent water and a pile of heavy stones weighing useless at the bottom. Eventually the stones pile higher and higher until the water is drowned. This is the truly amazing feat, the legacy of the 20th Century – the natural balance has been devastated, and we're told to be more concerned about share prices.

You assume that things can be changed. Would you agree that there's a certain altruism in what you do? That there's a sensibility out there that can be helped into a better way of thinking and doing?

We don't assume that things can change, only that people can change, and not to beat a path to the pay-off – another reason why some things are misunderstood, and our motives suspected. The motive should be clear. But everything has to be put on a plate these days without actually proposing anything different.

Touch is opening a few mental doors, but the assumptions behind magazines like The Face are not a altruistic – the motive purely commercial, and it's confirming, no long[er] shaping the values its readers have. Consume [...] consume me! Why are there so few others sha[...] your concerns – it's obvious that things are so bad [...] the moment that a certain altruism is not only nece[s]sary, but a prime responsibility for people work[ing] in magazines, the record business, all forms of m[e]dia.

I completely agree, but who would give up the [...] ted cow? I'm not so sure anymore whether The Fa[ce] shaped, confirmed, or just sat and watched its re[a]ders. I think a mixture of all three. As for altruis[m] there are plenty of people who share our concern[s] – the trouble is, you're having to compete with a pro[]cess that turns altruism into another commodity. Take U2, for example. They and countless others [...] do not seem to see this, and if they do, throwing the odd bit of money at a charity does next to nothing. Less, even.

That's exactly it – people have started out with good intentions, but they've been altered along the way without even knowing it. So altruism is not a fixed state, but a posture to be drawn upon whenever convenient.

But even when altruism is a fixed state, as you put [it] people are still incredibly suspicious, and a[ny] simple curiosity soon turns to cynicism if you do [not] make the appropriate noises.

Because we have achieved a high quality with the design and production of Touch, many assume that this is because we have a lot of money. The truth [is] that we started with a bank loan and have had to be careful with every penny. This is made more difficult when there is no advertising revenue to fall back on. Everything has to come from sales. We have no ba[n]ker – it has been our necks on the line financially and we cannot afford to pay ourselves anything. Ideally, we would all love to make the profits that would enable each of us to relinquish the often less-than-inspiring work we have to do in the meantime to pay the rent – we are no different to millions of ot[]hers. Some financial support would be great, but on what terms? So many people ask 'what must it be co[]sting you to do Touch?' For 'Ritual', we had to solicit the support of a typesetter, and a platemaker to do the colour printing. What it costs us is a lot of pa[]tience, care and time – the key to it.

Another problem is that our cover price, usually around that of an LP, is either too high („it's only a magazine") or too low (the more expensive, the more respected). Also, we give nothing in terms of reassurance, that is, promoting a lifestyle that everyone can identify with – or at least the so-called 'target audience', another example of communication as a collection of fragmented, self-regulating states. You cannot identify with Touch in the traditional way. It is working on a number of different levels, but one thing we are saying is find out about yourself, and identify with that'.

Isn't this the most frightening monster of all? Isn't modern capitalism based on the Idea that the majority are really dull and unsexy. You're turning the whole thing upside down. Is that why we're not in the Bahamas right now? Anyway, since you started doing Touch, what do you think about the way so much media has mushroomed in the mean[]time? Do you think the Media is now perceived as being a sexy thing, something ravishing that we're all meant to get involved with?

I don't think that at all – I suppose it's sexy if you think bondage is sexy. The Media is all about [...] version, and its environment, set in the West End of London or any major city, is polluted and corrupt. I know what you're saying – only a few years ago, angry young men and women whether sexy or not would form a band, but now they want to get in the media and start a magazine or be a TV presenter. Think of Jonathan Ross, host of the ironically-titled 'The Last Resort', which only started a few months ago. He is now a celebrity of sorts, and has been chosen to do the voice-overs for the AIDS warnings on Radio One. The most pressing problem facing young people's sexuality is focused by a chatshow presenter. He wears a nice clean suit. One of the big differences is that yesterday's heroes, people like Mick Jagger or John Lennon, caused parents to panic at the thought of their sons and daughters going anywhere near them. With Jonathan Ross, most parents would positively encourage such a contact – it would be good for their offsprings' careers. The Media is Britain's new manufacturing base, and we have openly welcomed the U.S.A.'s entertainment values and their policy of turning this country into a theme park – history island. So as for turning the whole thing upside down, what we'd really like to do is turn it the right way up. You can start by simply switching it off.

Are you not tempted to take a few interim measures?

What – to try other ways of marketing? We shall see what happens – there are plans afoot, not the least of which is to release more work separately in sound and print media, but the different products will be nonetheless related. We have projects underway with Z'ev, with the Hafler Trio, with a group from Newcastle called Pull who should by rights be at the top of the charts, folk music from Yugoslavia (some antidote to the truly dreadful Laibach is needed), and a series of printed pamphlets. I'd not think of any of them as 'interim measures' – in fact I hope we made the last of those some time ago. We are also just starting to work with a new group, Mother Tongue, which includes a great deal more than music: like an oral tradition.

We try to produce work that respects and doesn't patronise those that buy it, to promote active thoughts and feelings rather than to play the familiar games, however tried and tested. So we're not thinking of changing, simply looking for ways that we can make our energies more effective. But anything can happen, because everything is changing all the time.

Forms of communication involves certain limits, and it depends upon where you draw those limits. Most people in the media draw limits as to what they think the public will find acceptable, which usually translates into what best protects their vested interest. Over the last few years, the Thatcher Government has tightened its hold on all areas of the media. **We decided to draw the line that we were not going to let Touch become a vehicle for advertising, we were not Interested in style. We have never tried to resolve anything to do with style.** Work with The Hafler Trio, especially, has as little to do with style as it possibly could have. It's more to do with editing – the silent craft of the late 20th Century – but that's just from a technical viewpoint. Editing is a crucial part of everyday life – what you choose to react to, what you choose to ignore, and what slips in underneath.

If you walk down the street, the only way you ever know if somebody is into the same things as you are and the same thoughts as you are is if they're wearing the pointy shoes and sunglasses. We're all human, and we take our signals as we can find them, and that's been in the nature of revolutions for centuries, if I'm not mistaken. They rely on those 'man on the street' signals – the badges that you wear. What's going to happen if it isn't going to be like that anymore? How do we pick each other out?

You've got a very romantic idea of revolution. The revolution has to be one of perception. The disease is in perception, an inablitiy to read in the sense of not being able to engage, not being able to enter actively with another form or something you yourself have not directly experienced. You shouldn't forget about all your own direct experience in favour of some fantasy and easy escapism.

You should separate singer from song?

And of course vice-versa.

I'm really thinking of a 16 year old kid in a shopping mall in Akron, the equivalents of those who were moved by Punk and would have picked up on the records and all the visual signals. I had my life changed by such things ten years ago. Now, how can you get involved when you have this mesh that's refusing interaction?

In many ways, Punk was an accident – it could quite easily have been stifled at birth, but it was fortunate to have a few people at its heart who were A) very good organisers, especially of the media at that time and B) they were people who were not particularly interested in their own fame and fortunes. At the moment, the problem is that you have everybody waiting for 'the next big thing after Punk', but actually Punk was the last step before this style saturation we're now suffering. The powers that be – in this case multinational record company executives – won't let Punk happen again, and to protect their interests they pour masses of money into the advertising side of the business, everything to do with the presentation rather than content. This works in a similar way to how the United States force an arms race that the Soviet system cannot afford to keep up with. So with this 'revolution', you cannot talk about what 'the next step' will be – you have to think of the first step.

If you think of revolution in the way that you think of the Russian Revolution in 1917, you should remember that it took the bloodshed of the First World War for it to get to that stage. People think things are bad now, which for millions they are, but you could put up just as convincing an argument to say that things have never been better for most – the Thatcher argument, maybe, but you cannot ignore the fact. But where is the challenge to it? Things are so very well sewn up by the right wing, but my belief – well, I don't like the word 'belief' – my feeling is that they have got their sums badly wrong. They've underestimated people's love of nature. It needs somebody to focus this area with vision and good organisation – I think that's the revolution, because once you can understand that you are just a strand in the web of life, and act accordingly, everything else follows. For a start we need more women in areas of strong influence, not surrogate men like Margret Thatcher.

It is more difficult for us to do Touch at this moment because there is less of a support system than ever before. Independent distribution is in tatters. The masses get more apathetic, if that were possible. Others have retreated to sanctuaries, or persist in the belief of the next big thing – something that that might be 'about to happen'. Plenty is happening all the time. In experimental music and experimental art, everyone is played off against each other by the media as to who will be this next sensation. If that doesn't work, you can group artists and musicians together into some new cult, a 'school' or a 'movement' – what's going on in the New York art world at the moment with the 'Neo Geos'. **It's not often that you see art that useless. But in spite of all the rubbish, there are signs of other things. Networks are growing. Perhaps it's a race for two different visions of the millenium, full of paradoxes.**

A catalogue detailing Touch releases is available. Please write to TOUCH, 13 OSWARD ROAD, LONDON SW17 7SS, UK An IRC would be appreciated. Contributions are also welcomed for ‚Touch Language', whether sound, text or visual.

21

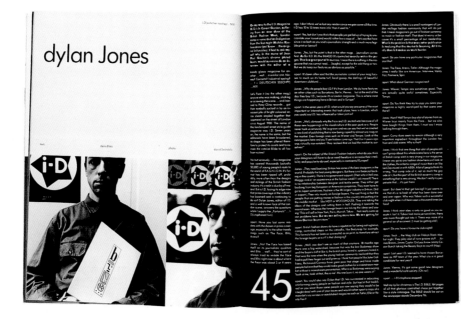

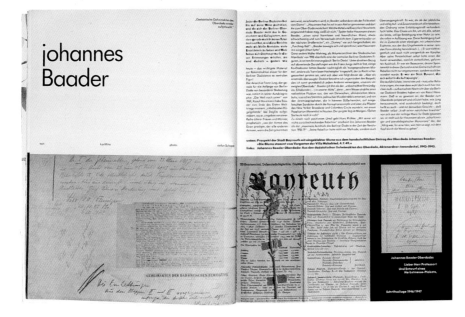

Apart *(Germany, Issue 10, 1988); 230 x 300mm*
As a reaction to the constantly changing trends of the mid-eighties, several issues of this culture magazine experimented with very rigid structures, testing at what point such a system becomes boring.
Art director *Mike Meiré*

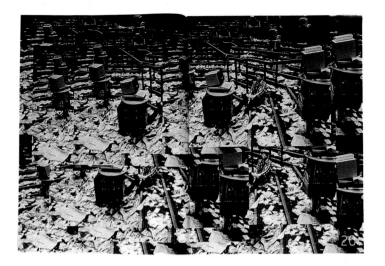

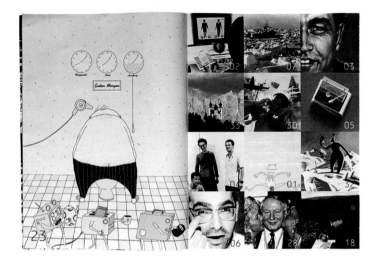

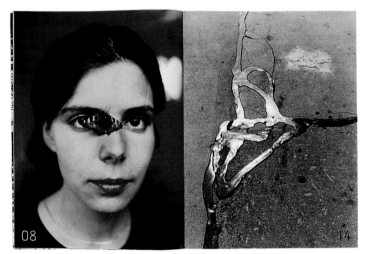

Delphine singen Schlager.

Geht es verständlich zu auf dieser Welt? Ganz bestimmt nicht. Jedenfalls nicht in Schweden. Dort wollte die Bürgerin Elizabeth Hallin ihren Sohn auf den Namen „Brfxxccxxmnpcccclllmmnprxvclmnckssqlbb11116" taufen lassen. Ein Bezirksgericht untersagte ihr das, unter Androhung einer Geldstrafe von umgerechnet tausend Mark. Frau Hallin geht jetzt in Berufung. Der Name, sagt sie, sei ihr während der Schwangerschaft als „künstlerischer Ausdruck einer expressionistischen Entwicklung" gekommen. Ausgesprochen wird der Name übrigens Albin (http://ucsu.colorado.edu/~robinsjr/New.html).

Wie der gute alte Nachname Koch jenseits des Atlantiks ausgesprochen wird, darüber gehen die Meinungen auseinander. New Yorks ehemaliger Bürgermeister bestand auf „Cotch", damit keiner auf dumme Gedanken käme. Sein Landsmann Frederick Koch aus dem County Windham, Connecticut, insistiert dagegen, „Coke" müsse das heißen. Nachdem er es leid war, die Leute ständig zu verbessern, beantragte er bei Gericht die Änderung seines Namens in „Coke-Is-It" und wird seitdem als Mr. It, Vorname Coke-Is geführt. Nicht mehr lange, denn die Firma Coca-Cola Inc. hat ihn wegen irreführender Verwendung eines Werbeslogans verklagt (http://www.milk.com/wall-o-shame/koch_is_it.html).

Klage, und zwar auf Schadensersatz in Höhe von sechzig Millionen Dollar, hat jetzt auch der amerikanische Fernsehstar Kermit eingereicht. Die Zeitschrift Bunte, so berichtet OTB-online, habe ein nichtautorisiertes Interview mit Kermit veröffentlicht, in dem er einräumt, mehr oder weniger steril zu sein und keine Kaulquappen zeu-

gen zu können. „Ich habe nie im Leben von diesem Bunte-Magazin gehört", wird der Kläger zitiert, „was denken diese Krauts, wer sie sind? Meine Sexualprobleme an die Öffentlichkeit zu zerren?" Kermit sei durch den Vorgang schwer verstört, heißt es dazu aus der „Sesamstraße", ein „mentales Wrack" und akut suizidgefährdet (http://www.ziplink.net/~zbrett/kermitkill.html).

Vieles ist offenbar nur eine Frage der Interpretation. Lange haben Wissenschaftler zum Beispiel darüber gerätselt, was die verschiedenen Laute der Delphinsprache bedeuten könnten. Bis der Delphinexperte Hector Corona auf die Idee kam, seine Tonbandaufzeichnungen mit einem Viertel der ursprünglichen Umdrehungszahl abzuhören. Ergebnis: Delphine singen sich gegenseitig aktuelle Schlager vor, die sie aus Radios aufgeschnappt haben. Auf Platz eins und zwei der Beliebtheitsskala: Mariah Carey und Bryan Adams (http://ucsu.colorado.edu/~robinsjr/New.html).

Das zeigt: Der clash of cultures muß nicht sein. Jedenfalls dann nicht, wenn man sich nicht so dämlich anstellt wie der Sportartikelhersteller Nike. Im Glauben, den besonders passenden Werbeträger gefunden zu haben, ließ die Firma einen alten Häuptling der kenianischen Samburu filmen, wie er ein Paar Nike-Schuhe in Empfang nimmt und dazu in der Stammessprache Maa wohlgesetzte Bemerkungen macht. Laut Untertitel angeblich „Just do it". In Wahrheit aber, so übersetzte ein Anthropologe der Universität von Cincinnati, fand der Häuptling folgende Worte: „Die will ich nicht. Gebt mir richtige" (http://www.milk.com/wall-o-shame/just_do_it.html).

Man muß sehr genau hinhören, in diesen babylonischen Zeiten.

Die virtuelle Umkleidekabine

machte Schluß mit Leistungssport und Psychoterror beim Einkaufen. Statt sich in muffigen Löchern während der Anprobe Arme auszurenken und von genervten Wartenden gehetzt zu werden („Mach hin, ey"), konnten die Kunden im Laden am Computer an ihrem Outfit herumfummeln. Figurdaten eingeben. Gesicht in die Kamera halten –

und schon turnte über den Bildschirm ein Kunst-Ich, allzeit bereit, per Fingerzeig in die wildesten Klamotten zu hüpfen. Die Idee der Kaufhof-Kette wurde weiterentwickelt. Alles wurde überflüssig: Verkäufer. Läden. Kleidung. Dann die Benutzer selbst. 2004 wurde der letzte echte Mensch gesichtet. Seither treffen sich unsere virtuellen Doppelgänger in schicken virtuellen Sachen an virtuellen Orten.

Oliver Kalkofe, Frustfresser, 32

Vor jeder Sendung von „Kalkofes Mattscheibe", die sonntags unverschlüsselt auf Premiere läuft, sieht man Sie vor einem Fernseher mit der Pumpgun über den Haufen schießen. Macht das Spaß?
Riesigen Spaß sogar. Es ist meine Rache am Fernsehen, weil es immer schlechter wird.
In Ihrer Satirereihe ziehen Sie seit viereinhalb Jahren über andere Fernsehmacher her – ohne Schlagersänger nennen Sie schon mal „Speckbulette" und Hans Meiser „Mümmelgreis". Was war Ihre liebste Beleidigung?
Da gab es viele, auch nonverbaler Art. Ich habe Leuten den Kopf weggesprengt oder sie komplett explodieren lassen – wir nehmen dafür Ausschnitte der Originalsendungen und bearbeiten sie am Computer. Den Moderator Jürgen Fliege habe ich zersägt, er verdiente das. Die meisten Leute nehmen meinen Humor zum Glück nicht persönlich.
Am liebsten ziehen Sie über Volksmusiker her und springen schon mal als falscher Heino mit Perücke ins Bild. Machen Sie es sich da nicht zu einfach?
Leider findet man spektakuläreren TV-Unsinn fast immer in der gleichen

Ecke. Viel lieber würde ich mich über Sabine Christiansen lustig machen, sie ist die Allerschlimmste. Ich habe lange nach einem entlarvenden Ausschnitt ihrer Talk-Show „Christiansen" gesucht. Da wird eine Stunde lang ins Nichts geredet, dieser Irrsinn läßt sich in der Kürze nicht vermitteln.
Was ist die schlechteste Sendung im deutschen Fernsehen?
Für den Titel gibt es unter den aktuellen Produktionen zwei Anwärter: die völlig konzeptlose Lottosendung auf RTL mit Günther Jauch, „Millionäre gesucht! Die SKL-Show", das ist Fernsehen wie in den sechziger Jahren, aber mit dem Geld von heute. Und „Perfect Day", auch auf RTL: Da spielen Leute darum, daß man ihre Schulden bezahlt. Was Zynischeres kann man sich kaum vorstellen.
Macht Fernsehen eigentlich dumm, wie viele glauben – oder einfach nur dick, wie man an Ihnen sieht?
Fernsehen ist schlimmstenfalls langweilig und frustriert die Fetzzellen. Ich sitze bei Premiere tagelang in einem abgedunkelten Zimmer, esse ab und zu was Süßes und spät abends dann richtig viel. Der Körper wehrt sich gegen den Mist in der Glotze. Man wird aus Verzweiflung dick.

Was zum Teufel ist mit dem ZEITmagazin passiert? Warum sind Texte und Bilder getrennt, welches Photo gehört zu welcher Geschichte? Keine Sorge, es ist alles in bester, wenn auch neuer Ordnung.

Alle Geschichten – von der Links-Kolumne bis zur Spielbank – finden Sie in der üblichen Reihenfolge auf den folgenden Seiten. Die unterlegten Zahlen verweisen auf die dazugehörigen Photos und Abbildungen im vorderen Heftteil.

Diese Struktur ist ein einmaliges Experiment der deutsch-österreichischen Agentur DMC (Design for Media and Communication), die wir gebeten haben, unser Computer Special zu gestalten. DMC hat vielen Fernsehsendern und -sendungen ein neues Gesicht gegeben, unter anderem auch der ARD und der „Tagesschau". Ihr Design greift immer wieder gut funktionierende Elemente und Mechanismen aus verschiedenen Kommunikationsfeldern auf und übersetzt sie für andere Medien, um dort eine größere Übersichtlichkeit und Benutzerfreundlichkeit zu erzielen. So verwenden die Designer etwa Ideen aus dem Printbereich oder der Welt der Computer im Fernsehen. Für unser Computer Special wollten wir wissen: Läßt sich die Internet-Logik auch sinnvoll auf das ZEITmagazin übertragen?

Im Ergebnis präsentiert sich die Titelseite mit dem Inhalt dieser Ausgabe wie eine Homepage. Innen hilft eine Menüleiste, die über jedem Text das Thema anzeigt, bei der Orientierung. Das Blättern zwischen Geschichten und Photos erinnert an das Klicken im World Wide Web, die verknüpfenden Zahlen sind die Links. Der radikale Bruch mit alten Lese- und Sehgewohnheiten macht nicht nur diese bewußter, sondern führt zu einer neuen Schau- und Leselust, dem erklärten Ziel von DMC-Chef Hubert Schillhuber:

„Als uns das ZEITmagazin zur Gestaltung des Sonderheftes Computer Special anläßlich der Cebit Home einlud, wurde unsere Kompetenz als Screendesigner gewünscht.

Was aber hat ein Printmedium mit Screendesign zu tun? Gibt es konvergierende Gestaltungstendenzen in beiden Medien? Oder kann gar mit kopernikanischer Kraft die Logik der interaktiven beziehungsweise bewegten Medien im Printbereich Geltung erlangen? Sieht man sich die zahlreichen Versuche in dieser Richtung an, bleibt der schale Geschmack von reiner Oberflächenbehandlung. Am ‚surface' aber

waren und sind wir immer nur in zweiter Linie interessiert. Zu trendgebunden und austauschbar ist der rein ästhetische Zugang in der Gestaltung. Also Konzentration auf die Funktion. Und die des ZEITmagazins heißt für uns Schaulust und Leselust!

Um dieses Ergebnis zu optimieren, haben wir von den Screenmedien die Dominanz des Bildes über das Wort übernommen und konsequent das Schauen dem Lesen vorangestellt (ein leichtes, dank traditionell hervorragender Photographie im ZEITmagazin).

Die strikte Trennung von Schauen und Lesen ermöglicht uns ein qualitativ anderes Wahrnehmungserlebnis. Jedem Part kommt ein höheres Gewicht zu als in jedem noch so ausgewogenen Layout. Bild und Text konkurrieren nicht mehr. Die Ergänzung (neudeutsch: der Hyperlink) findet zunächst in der Phantasie des Betrachters/Lesers oder – wenn gewünscht – tatsächlich statt. Die Verknüpfung von Text und Bild über ein Menü beziehungsweise Zahlenlinks ist keine Hommage an das Web, sondern pure Notwendigkeit der Benutzerführung, die es in jedem vernünftig gestalteten Printmedium auch gibt. Also nichts Neues. Oder?"

Der Österreicher Hubert Schilhuber, 40, gründete 1992 zusammen mit dem Londoner Graphik-Design-Star Neville Brody, 41, die Agentur DMC mit Sitz in Wien und Hamburg. Ihr erstes gemeinsames Projekt war die Entwicklung des Corporate Designs des Pay-TV-Senders premiere, der Anfang der neunziger Jahre mit den Konventionen der Fernsehästhetik brach. Klare Farbleitsysteme, einprägsame Logos und eine auf Funktionalität bedachte Schlichtheit gaben premiere eine moderne Identität. Wer heute durch die deutschsprachigen Kanäle zappt, kommt an den DMC-Arbeiten nicht mehr vorbei. Ob ARD, ORF, RTL 2 oder Viva – das Erscheinungsbild von insgesamt neun Stationen hat die Agentur bislang gestaltet. Dazu tragen TV-Magazine wie „Panorama" und „Kontraste" sowie Nachrichtensendungen wie die „Tagesschau", die „Tagesthemen" oder der „Bericht aus Bonn" ihre Handschrift.

PS: Pegasus '98 heißt der 3. Internet-Wettbewerb, den die ZEIT in Zusammenarbeit mit IBM, ARD online und Radio Bremen veranstaltet, der nach neuen Ausdrucksformen im Netz sucht. Einsendeschluß ist der 15. September. Infos gibt es unter www.pegasus98.de

---

brain

brain@novalink.com

your cranial control center need a little stimulation?

Mandatory Videogame: Play or No Pay

George Gets Back to Basics

Set-Top Studio

<Send> Dirty to Me

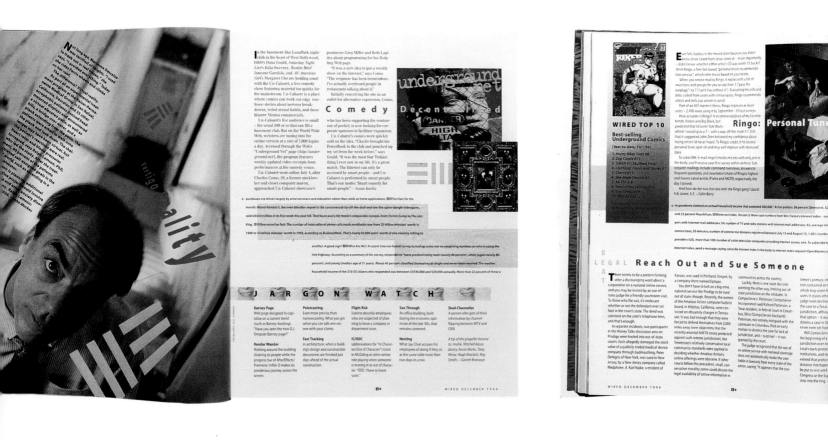

Comedy

JARGON WATCH

Ringo: Personal Tune

WIRED TOP 10 — Best-selling Underground Comics

Reach Out and Sue Someone

Smart Paper

TIRED

WIRED

SimSwim

Hot-Wired Braille Reader

Illuminating Geek Jokes

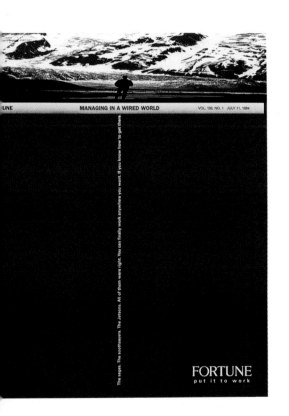
Wired (US, Issue 2.12, 1995) 230 x 275mm
In addition to the usual mix of short stories, the front section of this technology magazine, 'Electric World', includes a series of shorter stories and industry gossip that jumps from page to page.
Creative director *John Plunkett*

ANOTHER COUNTRY

BY Peter Atkins

'The Periodic Kingdom mainly consists of a metallic Western Desert, but

in the Eastern Rectangle is a softer, more colourful landscape whe

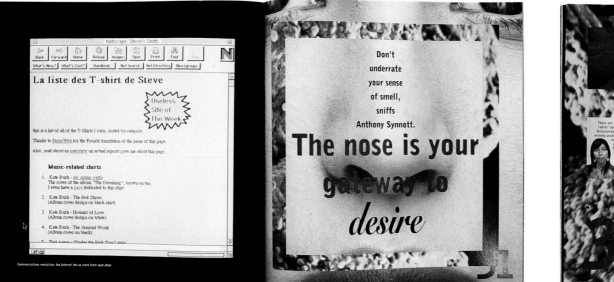

La liste des T-shirt de Steve

Useless Site of The Week

this is a list of all of the T-shirts I own, sorted by category.

Thanks to PezzoWeb for the French translation of the name of this page.

Also, read about an interview an actual reports gave me about this page.

Music-related shirts

1. Kate Bush - rec.music.gaffa
   The cover of the album "The Dreaming", brown on tan.
   I even have a page dedicated to this shirt

2. Kate Bush - The Red Shoes
   (Album cover design on black shirt)

3. Kate Bush - Hounds of Love
   (Album cover design on white)

4. Kate Bush - The Sensual World
   (Album cover on black)

Communication revolution: the Internet lets us learn from each other

Don't underrate your sense of smell, sniffs Anthony Synnott.

The nose is your gateway to *desire*

It takes one million petals to make a pint of rose oil

Silk Cut magazine ABOVE
(UK, Issue 1, 1996) 280 x 280mm

Silk Cut magazine BELOW
(UK, Issue 2, 1996) 280 x 280mm

Each issue of this magazine was based on a different theme. It was produced on behalf of a cigarette company and the publishers chose not to take advertising. As magazines rely on ads to break the run of editorial – they provide snappy, single-page breaks – this posed a problem. To get round this a series of single-page pieces was devised that not only helped the pace of the magazine but also reinforced each issue's theme: the first and last pages in the spreads shown are examples of these pages.
Art director *Jeremy Leslie*

ead, you deserve it

Adbusters (Canada, Issue 24, Winter 1999)
230 x 272mm

Adbusters is a non profit-making magazine concerned with the erosion of our physical and cultural environment by commercial forces. As such, it does not carry advertising, a fact which presents a challenge to the designer to maintain a rhythm and pace, but also frees up sites traditionally taken by advertising. In this example, a single message is run from the back cover, across the cover and on to the inside front cover.
Art director Chris Dixon

HOW

Reading Any 13 can be both a challenging and rewarding experience. While it may take a little getting used to, the application of the following simple reading tips will yield hours of reading and browsing pleasure for the entire family. If at any time you lose your way, don't panic! Simply look for one of the many markers and signposts that will surely get you back on track.

The essays examining the broader ideas of this issue read laterally along the top edge of the following pages. Here you will find writing by Georges Teyssot, Andrew Benjamin, and Luis Fernández-Galiano as well as an interview with Jacques Herzog and Pierre de Meuron.

To examine the competition entries submitted for the Tate Gallery of Modern Art by the six finalists, read along the middle of the page. Projects from the offices of Tadao Ando, David Chipperfield, Rafael Moneo, OMA, Renzo Piano, and Herzog & de Meuron are featured here and are clearly marked along the route.

A conversation between Cynthia Davidson, Nicholas Serota, and Richard Burdett runs perpendicular to the rest of the magazine. In order to read this dialogue tilt your head to the left so that your left ear approaches your left shoulder. If this position is uncomfortable or if neck cramping occurs, return your head to the full upright position immediately and proceed with this alternate method: turn the magazine clockwise 90 degrees so that the interview appears to read normally. Continue in this mode until you wish to return to the other texts, at which time you simply reverse the procedure and continue reading in the normal orientation.

13.21

READ
ANY 13
Tate Frames Architecture

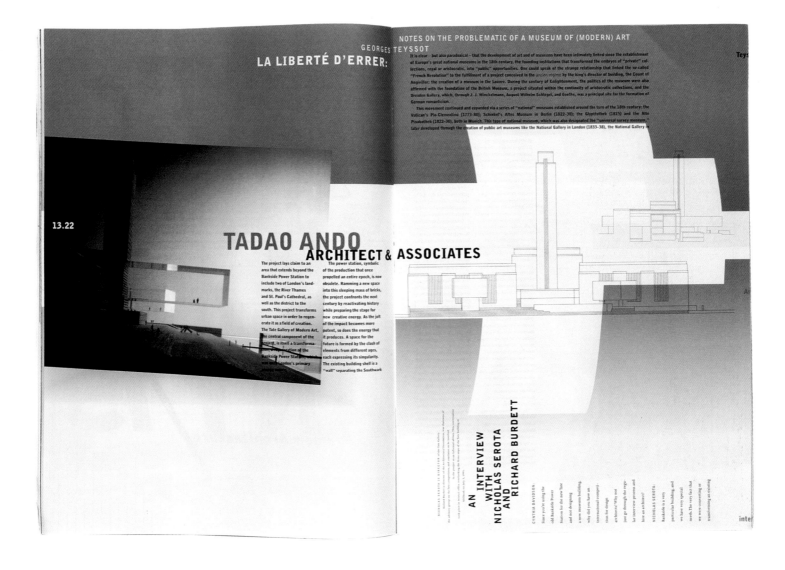

NOTES ON THE PROBLEMATIC OF A MUSEUM OF (MODERN) ART
GEORGES TEYSSOT

LA LIBERTÉ D'ERRER:

It is clear – but also paradoxical – that the development of art and of museums have been intimately linked since the establishment of Europe's great national museums in the 18th century, the founding institutions that transformed the embryos of "private" collections, royal or aristocratic, into "public" opportunities. One could speak of the strange relationship that linked the so-called "French Revolution" to the fulfilment of a project conceived in the *ancien régime* by the king's director of building, the Count of Angiviller; the creation of a museum in the Louvre. During the century of Enlightenment, the politics of the museum were also affirmed with the foundation of the British Museum, a project situated within the continuity of aristocratic collections, and the Dresden Gallery, which, through J. J. Winckelmann, August Wilhelm Schlegel, and Goethe, was a principal site for the formation of German romanticism.

This movement continued and expanded via a series of "national" museums established around the turn of the 18th century: the Vatican's Pio-Clementino (1773–80); Schinkel's Altes Museum in Berlin (1822–30); the Glyptothek (1815) and the Alte Pinakothek (1822–30), both in Munich. This type of national museum, which was also designated the "universal survey museum," later developed through the creation of public art museums like the National Gallery in London (1833–38), the National Gallery in

13.22

TADAO ANDO
ARCHITECT & ASSOCIATES

The project lays claim to an area that extends beyond the Bankside Power Station to include two of London's landmarks, the River Thames and St. Paul's Cathedral, as well as the district to the south. This project transforms urban space in order to regenerate it as a field of creation. The Tate Gallery of Modern Art, the central component of the project, is itself a transformation... of the Bankside Power Station, which was once London's primary

The power station, symbolic of the production that once propelled an entire epoch, is now obsolete. Ramming a new space into this sleeping mass of bricks, the project confronts the next century by reactivating history while preparing the stage for new creative energy. As the jolt of the impact becomes more potent, so does the energy that it produces. A space for the future is formed by the clash of elements from different ages, each expressing its singularity. The existing building shell is a "wall" separating the Southwark

AN INTERVIEW WITH NICHOLAS SEROTA AND RICHARD BURDETT

ANV (Architecture New York)
(US, Issue 13, 1996) 280 x 380mm

This issue featured a special 38-page report on plans for the new Tate Gallery in London. This was divided into three sections, which instead of being run consecutively were designed to run concurrently. Helping the reader cope with this break in convention took a whole spread of explanation, shown opposite, including a page-by-page breakdown of content, and the following explanation: 'essays examining the broader issues read laterally along the top edge... to examine the competition entries submitted by the six finalists, read along the middle of the page... a conversation between Cynthia Davidson, Nicholas Serota and Richard Burdett runs perpendicular to the rest of the magazine...'
Art director *Michael Rock*

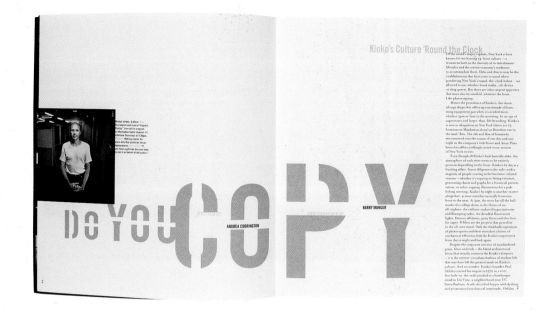

Rethinking Design *(US, Issue 4, 1997) 230 x 275mm*
These spreads from a feature about photocopy shops are designed to
build up pace as the feature progresses, while the increasing number of
photographs on each spread mimics the photocopying done in the shops.
Designers *Michael Bierut and Jacqueline Thaw, Pentagram*
Photographer *Barry Munger*

VISUAL \ CULTURE \ DOCUMENT   VOL 1 : NO 2

2wice

INTERIORS

Issue 2, Interiors

2wice *(US)*

'The lack of advertising means you have to give it its own sense of pace and rhythm.'

J. ABBOTT MILLER

MODERN DANCE BEGAN

when choreographers kicked off their ballet slippers and danced BAREFOOT on stage.

Along with their footwear, these early dancers—such as Loïe Fuller and Isadora Duncan—who abandoned the pointed toe as the standard measure of a dancer's movement, and in so doing cleared the slate for an entirely new vocabulary of twentieth century dance. By the 1960s, Martha Graham had created an elaborate language of highly expressive movement that depended on bare feet planted squarely on solid ground, and a decade later, Graham's student Merce Cunningham, focused his search for new movement on walking. Working with university students in 1952, Cunningham suggested that they begin with ordinary gestures—"These were accepted as movement in daily life, why not on stage?" he wrote—and he used the idiosyncratic pedestrian styles of each of them as the foundation for his choreographic design.

For dancers in the post-Cunningham era—from the early-sixties on—walking became the common denominator that linked their innovative experiments. Among the choreographers who formed The Judson Dance Theater in 1962, including Yvonne Rainer, Trisha Brown, Steve Paxton and Lucinda Childs, walking represented a radical stance against the dance establishment. It was a way of refuting the exclusivity of western dance forms and the suppression of individuality which its standards demanded. It was a way of democratizing dance, of insisting that anyone could be a dancer—"I envisioned myself

WALK ING

RoseLee Goldberg

as a post-modern dance evangelist bringing movement to the masses," Rainer wrote. And it was also a means for dance to serve as an accessible vehicle for social commentary, which by the late 1960s included reference to the tensions and nationwide anger provoked by the Vietnam War.

Dancers in the 1970s worked hard at making their movements look as natural and as close to everyday activities as possible. At the same time they attempted to foreground the process of art-making, often commenting on the mechanics of a particular movement as they danced. Their efforts paralleled the work of many conceptual artists of the period—Vito Acconci, Dennis Oppenheim, and Sol LeWitt among others—for whom the idea of art was as important as the actual execution of a work. Dance was used to investigate the meaning of the

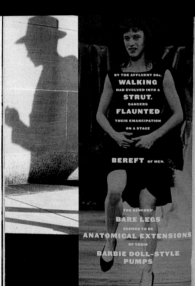

BY THE AFFLUENT 80s, WALKING HAD EVOLVED INTO A STRUT. DANCERS FLAUNTED THEIR EMANCIPATION ON A STAGE

BEREFT OF MEN.

THE DANCERS' BARE LEGS SEEMED TO BE ANATOMICAL EXTENSIONS OF THEIR BARBIE DOLL-STYLE PUMPS

form itself, and this highly conceptual approach erupted in a broad range of radical and compelling proposals. Trisha Brown devised a series of what she called equipment pieces to illustrate that dance is, in essence, a matter of gravity. In *Walking on the Wall* (1971), her dancers literally walked along the walls of a gallery, suspended from the ceiling by mountaineering equipment. Lucinda Childs used intricate notation to determine the paths her dancers would take, even as they increased the speed of their walking to the point at which they became airborne in a flurry of leaps and turns. Laura Dean, working from rigorous drawings that included an elaborate counting system, introduced a distinctive rhythm into her walk; performers stamped their feet severely, causing her modern dancers to spin in circles like ancient whirling dervishes. Dana Reitz, on the other hand, walked so slowly that watching her cross a stage was like viewing a series of Muybridge stills, where detecting changes in skeletal structure through repetition became the fascinating appeal of her work.

By the affluent 1980s, walking had evolved into a far more ambitious strut. The European walk, languorous and steep-heeled, distinguished the choreography of dancers on the eastern side of the Atlantic from their American counterparts. Pina Bausch's long-limbed dancers combined the edgy appeal of the streetwalker with the forceful precision of the highly trained dancer, with each step they relinquished a narrative thread into modern dance, creating, with their tautly configured strolling, vital ballets of longing and tenderness between male and female performers. Anne Teresa de Keersmaeker upped the

DANC ING

ante between the sexes, with a troupe of young female dancers who flaunted their emancipation on a stage bereft of men. The dancers' bare legs seemed to be anatomical extensions of their Barbie Doll-style pumps; despite the ridiculous arches of those shoes, they hit the ground running with fast-paced kicks and tumbles.

Such streetwalking could not be more different from the urban rhythms of America's streets and avenues. According to Jawole Willa Jo Zollar, of Urban Bush Women, "This country is more Africanized than we realize." Noting the subtle effects of African-American movement on the population at large—from tap and rock to double dutch and break dancing—Urban Bush Women created a series of ballets which incorporated the company's extensive research into African-American traditions. The 'shout dance,' which involves dancers shuffling

in a circle, actually dates back to sacred African ritual. Jane Comfort, on the other hand, compiled a repertoire of movements that reflected gender roles and specific ethnicities, which through repetition and rhythm became energetic and fluid dance. "Why do men always take up so much room?" "Why can't I spread my legs?" a female voice repeatedly asked over a sound track of rap rhythms, in a work where dancers seated themselves in a long row as though on an attached bench in a subway car. Moving through a pattern of positions uncannily familiar to any rider—the men leaning back, legs apart, and arms clasped behind their heads with elbows extended like bulls' horns from their shoulders, while the women wove their legs and arms together until their bodies looked like folded paper fans—Comfort created an exotic choreography from the colloquialisms of everyday body-language.

Having begun this walking tour, one is tempted to take off on quite another path, down the trail through art history. After all, landscape painting of the last century captured not only the beauty of the natural setting, but also the meandering route that took the artist there in the first place. More recently, the sculptor Richard Long made an art of it, walking on remote hilltops or across distant deserts, insisting all the while that his gallery exhibitions were mere detours from the splendors of actual physical landscapes. Performance artists Marina Abramovic and Ulay made a spectacular thousand-mile walk across the Great Wall of China in 1988; planned as a demonstration of will, and as a giant step across continents of varied cultures into the Chinese hinterland, their journey was also a remarkable dissertation on the art of walking.

In dance, performance, and the visual arts, walking heightens our perception of walking as a day-to-day experience, and points to our fallibility too. Laurie Anderson, in a song from *United States*, called "Looking for You; Walking and Falling," captures its essence: "You're walking. And you don't always realize it, but you're always falling....Over and over, you're falling. And then catching yourself from falling. And this is how you can be walking and falling at the same time."

RoseLee Goldberg, art historian, critic and curator, teaches at New York University and is a frequent contributor to *Artforum.*

ING

FALL

2wice

VISUAL \ CULTURE \ DOCUMENT
VOLUME 2 NUMBER 2

William H. Stockbridge
Photographer active 1900–1920
Cadets at the St. Louis World's Fair, 1904
Courtesy United States Military Academy Archives
West Point, New York

EDITOR IN CHIEF
Patsy Tarr

EDITOR/DESIGNER
J. Abbott Miller

MANAGING EDITOR
Paul Makovsky

DESIGN ASSOCIATES
Paul Carlos
Scott Devendorf
Design/Writing/Research, New York

CONTRIBUTING EDITOR
Nancy Dalva

ASSOCIATE EDITORS
Rika Burnham
William Harris

BUSINESS MANAGER
Jane Rosch

FOUNDATION ADMINISTRATOR
Michael Bloom

SYSTEMS ANALYST
Jeff Tarr, Jr.

PUBLIC RELATIONS
Nadine Johnson

ADVISORY BOARD
Victor Barcimanto
Geoffrey Beene
André Bishop
Lewis Black
Trisha Brown
Maria Calegari
Elaine Lustig Cohen
Bart Cook
Merce Cunningham
Julie Dale
James Danziger
Leon Dalva
Molissa Fenley
Audrey Friedman
Henry Louis Gates, Jr.
Dorothy Globus
Neil Greenberg
Barbara Horgan
John Jesurun
John Kelly
Wendy Keys
Salvatore La Rosa
Kevin MacKenzie
Richard Martin
Peter Martins
Mark Morris
Gregory Mosher
Patricia Pastor
Richard Peña
Stephen Petronio
Jean Pigozzi
Etheleen Staley
Elizabeth Streb
Paul Taylor
Twyla Tharp
Taki Wise

ACKNOWLEDGMENTS
Andre Balazs, Urshula Barbour, Geoffrey Beene,
Jill Bloomer, Conn Brattain, Carol Butler,
Sabine Breitweiser, Arthur and Alice Cloos,
Mathew Curlewis of the Ludlow Lounge,
John Corrigan, Fred Dennis, Howard Dillon,
Jane Duda, Candice Ferreira, Ron Gault,
Green-Naftali, Claire Gunning, Claire Jacobsen,
Nadine Johnson, Lisa Kahan, Steve Korte,
Peter Krueger-Christie's Foundation, Ellen Lupton,
Alycia Maudlin, Mercer Hotel, Annette Meyer,
Christian Muhr, Keri Murawski, Elizabeth Murphy,
Russell Nardozza, Todd Oldham, Walter Pamminger,
Gaylon Palotti, Kyong Park, Patricia Pastor,
Ruth Peltason, Irving Selero, Valerie Steele,
Hilary Strauss, Storefront for Art + Architecture,
Steve Van Dyk, Massimo Vignelli.

2wice
214 Sullivan Street
New York NY 10012
t 212 228 0540
f 212 228 0654
www.2wice.org
reply@2wice.org

ISBN 0–9657451–3–8

© 1998 2wice All Rights Reserved

PRINTED IN THE UNITED STATES BY
Hull Printing Company
63 Golden Street
Meriden, CT 06450
800 969 3300

DISTRIBUTED TO BOOKSTORES BY
Distributed Art Publishers
155 Sixth Avenue
New York, NY 10013 | 800 338 2665

COVERS
(front) Bodywrapp Inc. suit by Annette Meyec
1998. Photograph by Graham MacIndoe. Model:
Renee Keller from IMG.
(back and inside front cover) Bodywrapp suit
by Annette Meyer, 1998. Photograph by Graham
MacIndoe.

2wice® is published by the 2wice Arts Foundation, Inc.
Financial support is derived from individual and
foundation contributions and reader subscriptions.

2wice Arts Foundation, Inc., is a tax-exempt organization
under section 501(c)(3) of the Internal Revenue Code.
Contributions to 2wice Arts Foundation, Inc., are tax
deductible to the extent provided by law.

SUBSCRIPTION INFORMATION
one year $36 us $46 canada $56 foreign
two year $72 us $92 canada $112 foreign

To subscribe or to make changes to an
existing subscription, please write to:
2wice Arts Foundation
145 Central Park West
New York NY 10023

EDITORIAL QUERIES
We consider unsolicited submissions
but cannot return or respond to submissions that don't
include a self-addressed, stamped return envelope. For
more information, please send a self-addressed, stamped
envelope to: Guidelines, 2wice, 214 Sullivan Street
New York NY 10012

contents

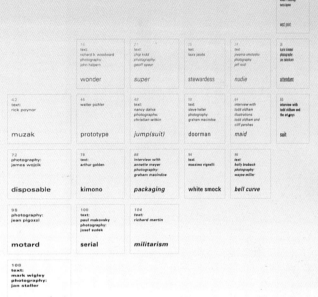

Issue 4, Uniform

Launched in 1997, each issue of *2wice* explores visual culture through a different theme. The design changes to suit these themes with each issue, the one common element being the care and attention with which it is designed by art director J. Abbott Miller. 'There is no house style or format,' he explains, 'Each issue responds to the theme. I usually start with the font Swift (as used on the logo) and move on from there.' He compares the magazine to a gallery or venue that is transformed for each new event or issue.

Unlike his other work on magazines such as *Architecture* (US) and *Guggenheim* (Spain), *2wice* is a non-commercial project, being funded by donation and subscription. It carries no advertising, which produces a particular challenge to the designer. In most magazines the ads provide a useful form of punctuation to the editorial, but as Abbott Miller points out, 'The lack of advertising means you have to give it its own sense of pace and rhythm'. This is done by carefully arranging the running order. In such a visually-led magazine this is crucial; the mix of photography and written material is carefully planned to exaggerate their differences and create variation of pace. Different issues have dealt with this in different ways: the first issue, 'Feet', used all manner of tricks to chop up the pace, including pages of printed trace paper and half-size pages, as shown opposite. This example, a history of modern dance, features a headline that builds as the orange half-

pages are turned, using the letters ING printed on the final page of the feature as a constant element. 'A nice rhythm,' is how Abbott Miller describes this, 'If I can connect things in this way I will.'

The fourth issue is much simpler in design; its theme, 'Uniform', lends itself to a very different interpretation. This issue works to a strict grid structure and exclusively uses Univers, giving it a very organized, uniform, feel. The contents page, shown above, is even laid out to mimic the textbook, diagrammatic representation of the weights of the Univers typeface. Abbott Miller sees this as perhaps the least successful edition of *2wice*. 'It worked well with the theme, but it was too cool.' The issues since have returned to the more free, eclectic style of Issue 1.

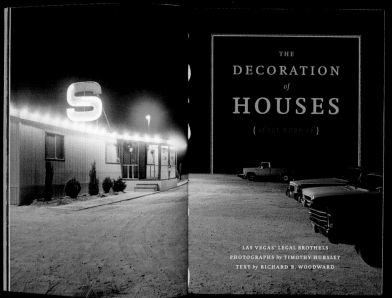

Issue 2, Interiors

Issue 3, Self

Issue 4, Uniform

Words

'You really have to understand about words – basically you're a journalist, you're expressing meaning.'

MARK PORTER, THE GUARDIAN

Computer technology liberated the magazine designer overnight. Previously, not only the perceived need for legibility and reader familiarity, but also the combined demands of typesetting production and deadlines created the need for simplicity and regularity. With the introduction of the Apple Mac, total control over the appearance of every word in a publication was available to the designer.

At the beginning of the nineties with *Beach Culture* (US) and later with *Raygun* (US) David Carson took full advantage of the new technology, pushing what was permissible in a magazine until it all but collapsed. With the exception of early, pre-Mac issues of *i-D* (UK) no one had so deliberately attacked legibility. Polarizing opinion in magazine offices across the world – editors hated it, art directors loved it – Carson continued breaking down the conventions of editorial design until by the time he left the magazine in 1995 there was nothing left to try: *Raygun* had become the latest style fad.

In a wider context, Carson's work on *Raygun* can be seen as part of a recent tradition in US magazine design, an approach that sets it apart from European magazines. US magazines such as *Rolling Stone* and *Entertainment Weekly* have established an exuberant graphic style that changes from story to story. These are the opposite of minimalism, which is perceived on both sides of the Atlantic as a European trait. 'In America there remains the lingering influence of David Carson, Fred Woodward and Fabian Baron, designers who vary and adapt, using the typographic gesture,' explains American art director J. Abbott Miller, 'while in Europe there is a lingering interest in system and structure; not fundamentalist Bauhaus but a strictness I don't relate to but enjoy.' When Robert Newman joined *Details* (US) as art director, part of his brief from the editor was to '…make a sharp break with the

past, which was very modernistic typography with a European feel. He wanted it to be very much an American-feeling mag.' Newman achieved this by using various American cultural references, notably Blue Note record sleeves and seventies typography.

Such references are a major part of American magazine design. *Speak* (see page 143) takes its typographic inspiration from items collected by its art director. Fred Woodward, art director of *Rolling Stone*, recalls his regret that a particular typeface he had used on a spread in the magazine was 'too trendy'. Instead he prefers to work with the writer's words and the photographer or illustrator's images, choosing typefaces and designs to interpret and complement respectively. 'I think there is a perfect use for every godawful typeface ever drawn and it's my mission to do so before I die.' Woodward gives himself and his team a free rein with typefaces and design. Consequently *Rolling Stone* has no specific style, as Woodward admits: 'If there's any kind of style at all at *Rolling Stone* it's what my editor once described as "big words on a page".' He uses design to make the editorial stand out from the ads, treating the openers to features '…like posters or book covers and less as conventional editorial pages'. Thus, features look very different to each other and make reference to a variety of sources.

By contrast, European magazines generally keep faith with modernism, the designer preferring to work to a pre-set group of formats and styles. Inevitably this is a generalization – some American designers such as Gary Koepke are clearly working to the European model – but it does describe the difference between most magazines either side of the Atlantic. British designers Chris Ashworth and Neil Fletcher took over as art directors on *Raygun* and tried to bridge this gap, 'We were very influenced by David Carson but wanted to move the design along. We

didn't introduce a rigid grid but we did bring a simpler approach to the magazine, adding a European typographic rigour to the edgy grunginess of *Raygun*. We called it Swiss Grit.' Both approaches took different advantage of type technology: Carson relied on the inventiveness of the young type designers who sent him their latest faces, while Ashworth and Fletcher would scan damaged Letraset characters and create fonts using the Fontographer program.

Whichever style they follow, however, the basic elements remain the same: the magazine-literate reader expects a headline and a standfirst followed by the text. Even David Carson's work acknowledges this. His final issue of *Raygun* was typical of his work on the magazine; while rendering the words difficult to read, he was also displaying a knowledge and understanding of how a magazine works. In this case the dominant words at the start of every article are headline-sized labels such as Author, Photographer, Quote. Irrelevant to the reader, but key to the structure of any layout, they hint at the regular set of parts that make up a page at the start of an article: the headline, the intro, the picture, the credits, and finally the text itself. It is the way that these parts are designed and combined, the way these words interact, that gives a magazine its character.

Gary Koepke's work for *Vibe* (US) is a good example of how these elements can be combined in different ways to different effect (see page 120). Using two typefaces, one for the headline, one for all other text, the changes in scale and position of the various elements give entirely different moods to the pages.

British designer Mark Porter sees himself as being 'in charge of the distribution of elements in space.' He starts a page design by choosing a picture, decides its scale, position and crop, then adds the type. 'You can take these elements – the image, the headline and the standfirst – and

Words

arrange them differently and it always amazes me how much their meaning can change.' As art director of the *Guardian* newspaper's magazine *Weekend* (UK), he has created an uncluttered design that he describes as 'European modernist ranged left, sans serif'. He wants the design to go unnoticed, believing that it often gets in the way of the message: 'We want the readers to see the ideas and words not the design', he explains, 'If people notice the design we've failed.'

J. Abbott Miller has a similar aim but comes at the problem from a very different angle. With projects such as *2wice* (US), *Architecture* (US) and *Guggenheim Magazine* (US) he has been attempting to get the type to be not just sympathetic in style but also in placement and attitude. 'With *2wice* I want to merge the subject and the artifact, to remove the 'frame' of the magazine and go straight to the meaning.' *Architecture*, meanwhile, features innovative use of technology to combine image and type, resulting in clear, simple typography that enhances the imagery instead of competing with it.

As Porter points out, typography is one area in which magazine designers feel they have a licence to play. 'A lot of big-name magazine designers – David Carson, Fabian Baron – have been very powerful typographers. There is a pressure to design with type, but anything that interferes with the story is bad.'

Art director team Lee Swillingham and Stuart Spalding at *Dazed & Confused* (UK) resist the temptation to overpower the imagery they have so carefully worked on with photographers, but stress the need for identity; 'The magazine must be more than a photographer's portfolio – we want a voice through the graphics too.'

Porter's approach is a strong one but one that is spreading. Now that technology has given full control over type to the designer it is easier for people to 'interfere with the story'. The experiments of *i-D* and *Raygun* have gone mainstream and now the new, cutting edge magazines worship simplicity. Publications such as *SleazeNation* (UK), *Econy* (Germany) and *Flaunt* (US) all rely on clean, minimalist typography. Even *i-D* has changed its approach, using a deliberately simple, undesigned style, as founder and creative director Terry Jones explains: 'At present legibility and communication are the most important factors as we're aiming to make *i-D* a global magazine.'

TOP **i-D** *(UK, June 1987) 210 x 280mm*
Art director *Terry Jones*
Photographer *Jamie Long*

BOTTOM **i-D** *(UK, September 1998) 230 x 300mm*
Art director *Kate Law*
Creative director *Terry Jones*
Photographer *Juergen Teller*

i-D, perhaps uniquely, has remained at the cutting edge of magazines since its inception as a fashion fanzine in 1979. During the eighties it experimented with layering type – pushing the boundaries of legibility in a way that foresaw David Carson's work for *Raygun* – a process founder and creative director Terry Jones describes as 'slowing the reader down'. The magazine's current priorities have changed completely, legibility and communication now being seen as all-important.

bryan ferry

photos:Peter Morello stylist: Jill Spector

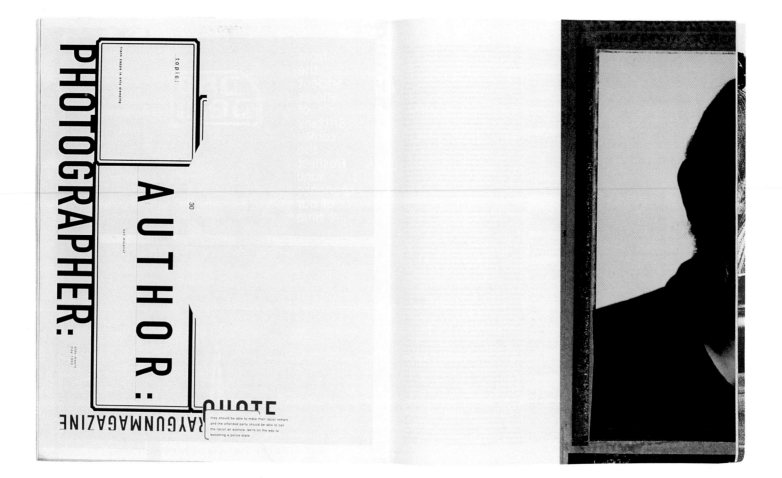

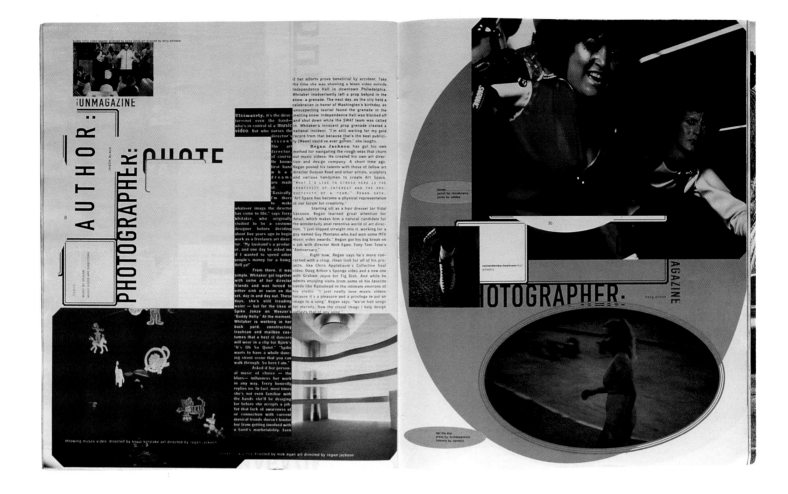

PREVIOUS SPREAD **Raygun** (US, Issue 21, 1994) 250 x 305mm
Extreme *Raygun*: this interview was deemed so dull that it was designed
using the symbol font Zapf Dingbats.
Art director *David Carson*

THIS SPREAD **Raygun** (US, Issue 30, 1995) 250 x 305mm
The issue that saw the relationship between David Carson and *Raygun*
publisher Marvin Scott Jarrett finally break down, Issue 30 labelled all
the major graphic elements on each page with their generic title. These
labels were designed as the prominent feature, appearing far larger than
the information to which they referred. The two spreads shown opposite
are a profile of Frank Zappa (TOP) and an interview with David Bowie
(BOTTOM). The subjects' names are printed in 8pt while the labels
AUTHOR, PHOTOGRAPHER and QUOTE dominate in large, bold capitals.
The example on this page shows the chaos caused when this system is
applied to a spread with several shorter pieces.
Art director *David Carson*

END GAMES

People of the next century
will gaze back with ghastly awe
upon our time...
a time of waste and abandon on a scale so
vast it knocked the planet out of
whack for a thousand years

THIS PAGE **Adbusters** *(Canada, Issue 23, 1998) 228 x 272mm*
This magazine deals with the erosion of our physical and cultural environment by commercial forces. Given this subject matter its appearance might be expected to be dull and worthy; instead it utilizes the language of magazines to present its argument in a form that does not just preach to the converted. In this example the type has been combined with collaged imagery to produce a disjointed and rough style that reflects the non-traditional visual journey the reader will experience in the following feature.
Art director *Chris Dixon*

OPPOSITE, TOP **Utne Reader** *(US, Issue 68, 1995) 194 x 254mm*
This headline mixes typeface and found type, in the form of a photograph of the word 'Music'.
Design *Jan Jancourt and Andrew Henderson*

OPPOSITE, BOTTOM **EU** *(UK, Pilot issue, 1993) 230 x 300mm*
Although it never went into production, this prototype pan-European magazine for language students successfully combined regular typefaces with found type such as metal stencils.
Art director *Phil Bicker*

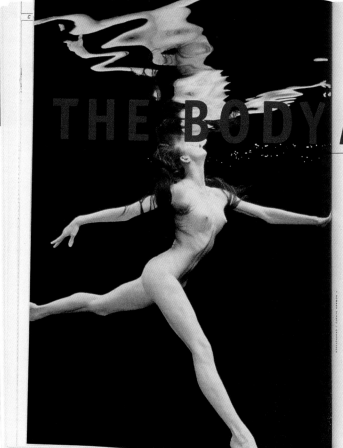

THE BODY AS

AUSTRALIAN WELLBEING
Larry Dossey.

*Achieving great
tone without exercise*

Many living organisms communicate so richly through sound that it is hard to imagine their surviving without it. In many species the life-sustaining processes of mating and reproduction rely solidly on systems of calls—bird song and the songs of whales are examples—that are bewilderingly complex and in some cases decidedly musical. Sound and the continuation of life go hand in hand.

In humans, the physical body reflects the sound we perceive, down to the biochemical level. We are so sensitive to sound that noise pollution has been called the most common modern health hazard. High levels of unpleasant sounds cause blood vessels to constrict; increase blood pressure, pulse, and respiratory rates; release extra fats into the bloodstream; and cause the blood's magnesium level to fall.

People are disturbed not only by loud sounds but also by sounds that are dissonant or inharmonic. They can also be disturbed by silence. If healthy persons are confined to bed and exposed to soft but varied harmonic sounds, they perceive their environment as more restful than do subjects who are in a completely quiet environment.

Yet sounds can mean something to us that is not adequately explained by an analysis of the physical changes they cause. Some are tied to spiritual or religious experiences, which are distinct from the physical processes of mating, reproduction, species survival, and body chemistry.

For millennia, great spiritual traditions have prescribed the repetition of certain sounds that promote the experience of transcendent realities. The ritualistic use of specific chants, prayers, incantations, affirmations, and holy words is worldwide. Are these sounds affecting our spiritual health, just as other sounds can affect our physical health? Could certain sounds affect both our physical and spiritual well-being?

There is evidence for this possibility. Certain meditation practices that emphasize the repetitious chanting of special sounds, or mantras, are associated with demonstrable health benefits. For example, transcendental meditation, which employs mantras, has been helpful in treating medical problems such as irregular heart rhythms. And statistics show that the rate of hospital admissions and the overall health costs of practitioners of the technique are lower than those of nonmeditators.

Although we ordinarily think silence excludes sound, certain sounds can be helpful, paradoxically, in coming to the Great Silence, or the mystical experience of "oneness," of which all the major spiritual traditions speak.

Cultivation of silence has also been shown to have positive health benefits. In one study, when men with high blood cholesterol levels learned to quiet their mental activity for 20 minutes twice a day while simply sitting in a chair, their cholesterol levels fell by one-third.

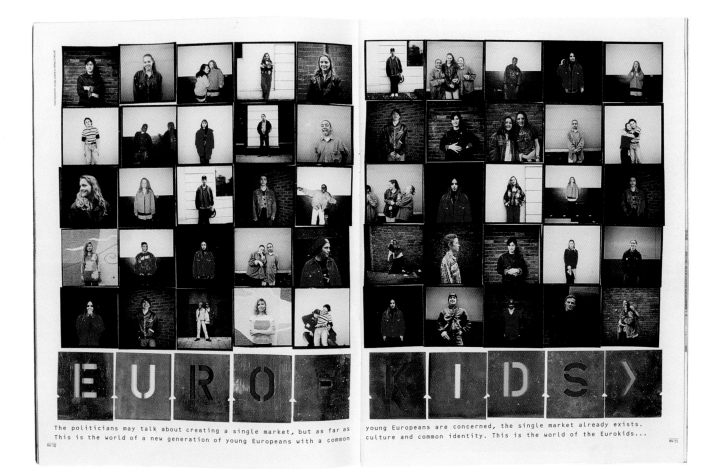

E U R O - K I D S ›

The politicians may talk about creating a single market, but as far as young Europeans are concerned, the single market already exists. This is the world of a new generation of young Europeans with a common culture and common identity. This is the world of the Eurokids...

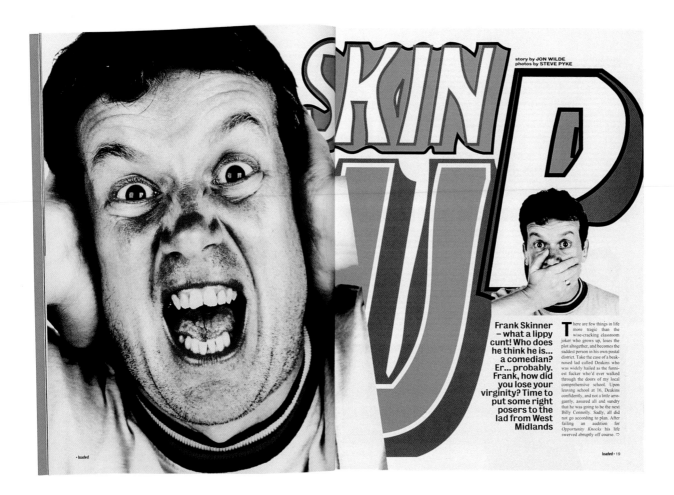

story by JON WILDE
photos by STEVE PYKE

SKIN UP?

Frank Skinner – what a lippy cunt! Who does he think he is... a comedian? Er... probably. Frank, how did you lose your virginity? Time to put some right posers to the lad from West Midlands

There are few things in life more tragic than the wise-cracking classroom joker who grows up, loses the plot altogether, and becomes the saddest person in his own postal district. Take the case of a beak-nosed lad called Deakins who was widely hailed as the funniest fucker who'd ever walked through the doors of my local comprehensive school. Upon leaving school at 16, Deakins confidently, and not a little arrogantly, assured all and sundry that he was going to be the next Billy Connolly. Sadly, all did not go according to plan. After failing an audition for *Opportunity Knocks* his life swerved abruptly off course. ⏎

water sports story by TIM SOUTHWELL photos by NEALE HAYNES

hawaii

FIVE OH!

When the world's swashbuckliest pro windsurfer invites you for a weekend of free lessons, shark baiting and pina colladas thrown over you by beautiful women in bikinis, you can hardly say no can you?

It's 6.30am (that's AM!) and I'm standing (that's upright!) on Kanaha beach on the Hawaiian island of Maui with Nik Baker, one of the best windsurfing wave riders in the world. It's his 24th birthday and he should be in bed getting rid of last night's party hangover under the soothing guidance of his fine lady or be out at Hookipa beach ripping the shit out of big waves. Whichever way you look at it, he's suffered a ⏎

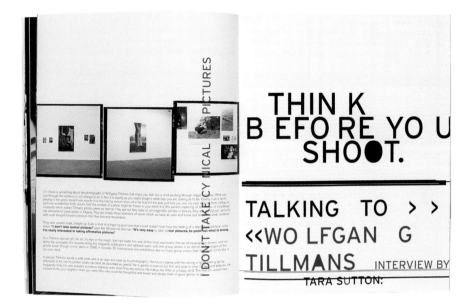

THINK
BEFORE YOU
SHOOT.

TALKING TO >>
<<WOLFGANG
TILLMANS   INTERVIEW BY
TARA SUTTON:

I DON'T TAKE CYNICAL PICTURES

"I AM A DJ I AM WHAT I PLAY
I'VE GOT BELIEVERS BELIEVING ME."
>>DAVID BOWIE

DaWN oF
ThE DJ
StORY BY MarINA FahSBENDeR:
PaINTING By JaCK FEaTHerLY:

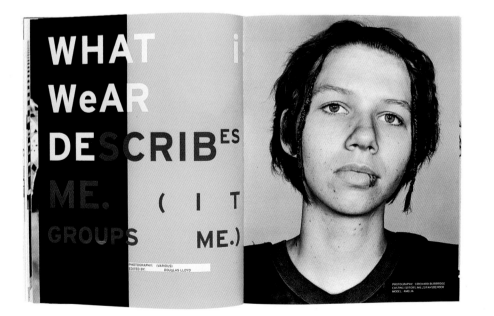

WHAT   i
WeAR
DESCRIBes
ME.
(IT
GROUPS   ME.)

PHOTOGRAPHY: (VARIOUS)
EDITED BY: DOUGLAS LLOYD

PHOTOGRAPHY: CRICHARD BURBRIDGE
CASTING EDITORS: MILLS/FAHSBENDER
MODEL: AMELIA

OPPOSITE PAGE   **Loaded** *(UK, October 1994, July 1995) 220 x 295mm*
One of the publishing success stories of the nineties,
Loaded helped create the new genre of 'lad' magazine.
Primarily concerned with football, lager and sex, it had to
look like it didn't care about its appearance. To achieve this
the design took full advantage of the surface style of David
Carson's *Raygun* and of the then new technology, creating
a look that was heavily designed to look undesigned.
Art director *Steve Read*

THIS PAGE   **Big** *(US, Issue 19, 1998) 240 x 305mm*
A simple but distressed treatment of type, referring to old-
tech stencils, gives this issue its own character.
Art director *David Lloyd*

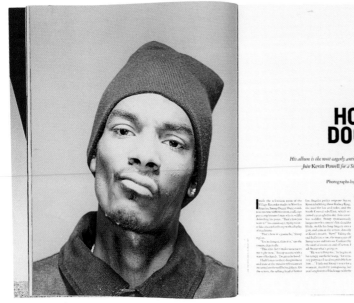

HOT DOGG

His album is the most eagerly anticipated debut in hip hop history.
Jate Kevin Powell for a Snoop Dogg-day afternoon.

Photographs by Dan Winters

September 1993

OF
PHREAKS
AND
HACKERS

A brief sojourn among the young sultans of software and
captains of code before the info highway paves this underground over.
By Carol Cooper. Illustrations by John Hersey

June/July 1994

September 1993

THIS PAGE **Vibe** *(US) 250 x 305mm*

Three spreads from this urban culture magazine demonstrate how powerful and flexible a single headline font can be. The top example uses the blue from the portrait to highlight the extra G in what otherwise is a very simple and spacious start to a feature; the middle spread goes to the other extreme, using scale to shout the words; the bottom example takes advantage of the cramped two-page feature to use the type to echo the picture.
Art director *Gary Koepke*

OPPOSITE PAGE **Raygun** *(US, October 1997, November 1997) 250 x 305mm*

These designs show the successful attempt by two English designers to move *Raygun* on while remaining true to David Carson's original concept. Legibility remains a low priority, but the Mac-based font designs and deconstruction of Carson is replaced by a deliberate attempt to look as un-Mac generated as possible. A damaged Swiss typographic feel is introduced ('dirty Swiss') and headlines created by scanning in characters from old Letraset sheets.
Art directors *Chris Ashworth and Neil Fletcher*

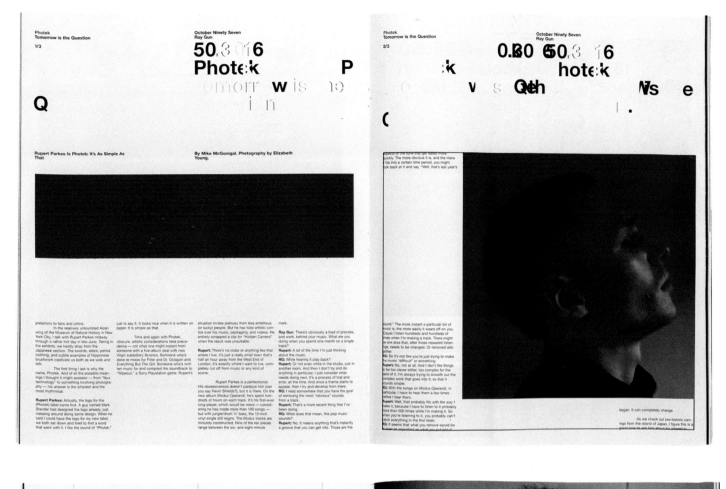

50.3016
Photek
Q

Rupert Parkes Is Photek: It's As Simple As That

By Mike McGonigal. Photography by Elizabeth Young.

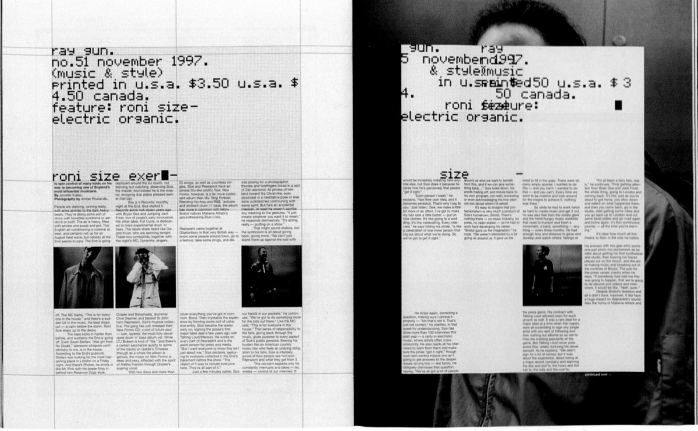

NEWYOrK

Williamsburg Bridge, 1947.

New York is a city of perspectives. They are as clearly visualised as in the little Palladian theatre at Vicenza. The distances are as sharp as the foreground. The streets are straight tunnels beneath mountainous buildings and, with their metal kerbs and tarmac or concrete surfaces, the noise which reverberates from them is unlike that of any other city.

Donatella Versace, by Steven Meisel.

She may appear to be an archetypal Versace woman, but Donatella, Gianni's sister and indeed his active inspiration, is far more than mere designer's muse: she's been described as the "engine room" of the whole Versace thing. Viewed by one of the masters of the art of portraiture, Steven Meisel, who exposes in these pages all her alluring and enigmatic beauty.

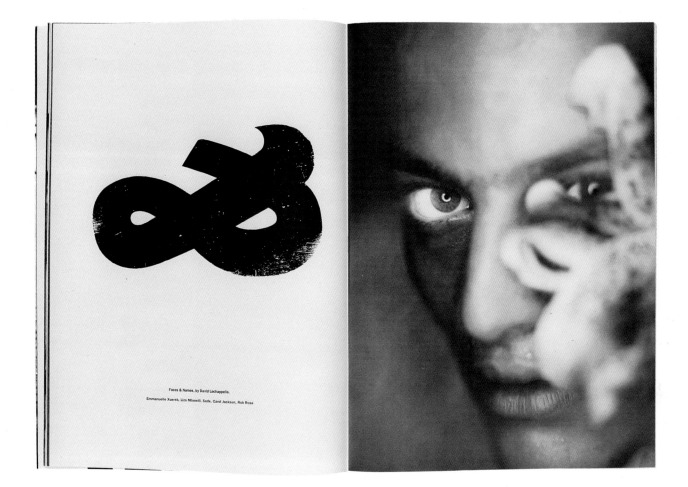

Faces & Names, by David Lachappelle.

Emmanuelle Xuereb, Liza Minnelli, Sade, Carol Jackson, Rob Rosa

Big *(Spain, New York issue) 297 x 410mm*
Wood block type is used to provide a visual echo of both New York and of the black and white photography in this large-format magazine. This combination became the magazine's identity.
Art director Vince Frost

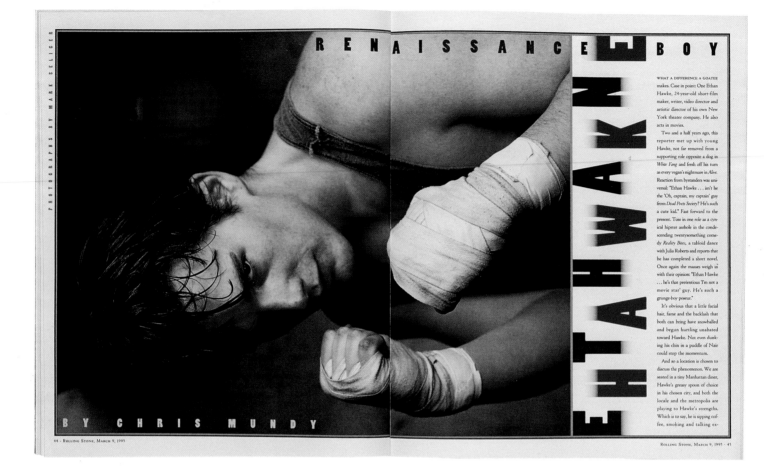

ETHAWKE

BY CHRIS MUNDY

WHAT A DIFFERENCE A GOATEE makes. Case in point: One Ethan Hawke, 24-year-old short-film maker, writer, video director and artistic director of his own New York theater company. He also acts in movies.

Two and a half years ago, this reporter met up with young Hawke, not far removed from a supporting role opposite a dog in *White Fang* and fresh off his turn as every vegan's nightmare in *Alive*. Reaction from bystanders was universal: "Ethan Hawke . . . isn't he the 'Oh, captain, my captain' guy from *Dead Poets Society?* He's such a cute kid." Fast forward to the present. Toss in one role as a cynical hipster asshole in the condescending twentysomething comedy *Reality Bites*, a tabloid dance with Julia Roberts and reports that he has completed a short novel. Once again the masses weigh in with their opinion: "Ethan Hawke . . . he's that pretentious 'I'm not a movie star' guy. He's such a grunge-boy poseur."

It's obvious that a little facial hair, fame and the backlash that both can bring have snowballed and begun hurtling unabated toward Hawke. Not even dunking his chin in a puddle of Nair could stop the momentum.

And so a location is chosen to discuss the phenomenon. We are seated in a tiny Manhattan diner, Hawke's greasy spoon of choice in his chosen city, and both the locale and the metropolis are playing to Hawke's strengths. Which is to say, he is sipping coffee, smoking and talking ex-

LOST IN SPACE

OUTLAW ENGINEERS ARE STRUGGLING TO SAVE NASA WITH A NEW GENERATION OF SECRET TECHNOLOGY

BY LAURENCE GONZALES

IN A CONCRETE ROOM off Building 30's entrance, a guard with a gun gave me an ID badge and a four-digit code. We crossed the lobby, and I had to stick my hand inside a dark box and enter my code on a touch pad while a sign instructed me to look into the mirror and a camera scanned my face. A shiny steel door swung open. I was in. ★ A sign inside said WARNING! THIS IS AN OPERATIONS SYSTEM USED FOR SPACE SHUTTLE SUPPORT. DO NOT TOUCH ANYTHING! In this building, which is painted the color of uncooked pasta and smells like a school cafeteria, the business of Mission Control has gone on since the Gemini and Apollo days. ★ I plunged through corridors of humming equipment. Everywhere old green steel cabinets full of antique wiring were being ripped out and replaced by smaller, molded sculptures of lustrous plastic filled with integrated circuits. At no time in history will the revolution that is going on inside NASA be more evident than it is now, in the guts of the Control Room. ★ On one side of a great cavernous room were the old-fashioned telephone-patch bays, a Medusa of wires curling to the floor, dozens of quaint silver computer-tape reels nervously stopping and starting, wooden skids of spent tapes stacked around, miles of paper spewing from immense line-printing machines, downlink monitor numbers clicking over on the shabby monochromatic screens cased in steel like old Army-tank parts. ★ On the other side of the room were new high-speed disk drives, robotic 85-gigabyte tape-cassette machines and brilliant color monitors screaming with a faint supersonic whine through train loads of numbers. The 1.2-terabyte "jukebox" contained the recorded data from every shuttle mission ever flown, all stored on optical disks in this Sony Writable Auto Disk changer. A group of seven boxes, each 4 feet tall, had replaced an entire building full of tapes. ★ I couldn't help wondering if the astronauts in the shuttle mission STS-59, which at that moment was flying 120 miles up over Lake Superior, understood that their delicate craft was being buoyed aloft as this tangled gob of wire was

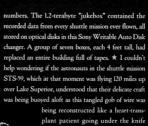

being reconstructed like a heart-transplant patient going under the knife while the operating room is rebuilt around him. ★ Escorted by John Muratore, I passed among the scores of people working control- and technical-backup positions. In the revolution that has been quietly taking place at NASA, Muratore is the Che Guevara. Now 38, Muratore started his campaign more than a decade ago when he discovered that his home laptop could do things that Mission Control's computers could not. But the putsch turned into a desperate effort to rescue the space agency from extinction. To that end, Muratore and a handful of young engineers who called themselves the Pirate team waged an unrelenting and clandestine guerrilla war against the bloated and stultifying NASA bureaucracy. The Pirates literally had to tear apart the computers that ran the place and take control from the ground up. The amazing thing is that they did it all in nearly total secrecy — operating through back channels, meeting at midnight, scrounging for equipment and skating on the edge of legality. After staging a virtual takeover of one of the world's most elite technical agencies, the Pirate

OPPOSITE **Rolling Stone** (US, Issue 21, 1994) 250 x 305mm

THIS PAGE **Rolling Stone** (US, Issue 30, 1995) 250 x 305mm

This fortnightly music magazine has developed an influential free style that relies on the words for inspiration. The Ethan Hawke story turns the picture on its side to extract maximum scale and give a poster feel to the spread. This feel is enhanced by the 'jumping' type, which also relates to the boxing imagery of the portrait. The type for 'Lost In Space' is typical Rolling Stone: a gently futuristic font is used to create a graphic interpretation of the words. Art director Fred Woodward

Words
125

POWER PLAY

An exclusive report reveals how the Russian mob has muscled its way into the NHL—and fouled some of hockey's biggest stars
By Robert I. Friedman

Connected (from top): The Vancouver Canucks' Pavel Bure; **mobster Vyacheslav Ivankov in FBI custody;** Detroit Red Wings and other Russia Reiters.

DONETSK, A BLEAK INDUSTRIAL CITY IN THE SOUTHEAST CORNER of the Ukraine, is not known for producing hockey players. And when Oleg Tverdovsky, a scrawny seven-year-old, tried out for a local peewee team, he didn't show much promise. His ankles were weak—the result of a joint-swelling disease called Reiter's syndrome—and he was one of the worst skaters in the bunch. At first, he didn't even like the sport much. Still, a coach spied some potential in him and encouraged the boy to keep at it.

He did. By sixteen, Tverdovsky had blossomed into one of the highest-scoring defensemen in Russia, playing for a team called the Soviet Wings. But with the fall of Communism, Soviet hockey also collapsed. Arena freezers frequently broke down, melting the ice. Stadiums that once drew five thousand fans were lucky to lure several hundred. "People had a lot of problems in ➡

Oh My GoD! THeY MaDe A MoViE!

They're the evil twins to Damon and Affleck. A year ago,
MATT STONE and TREY PARKER were living on cocktail wienies.
Now, the two creators of South Park *have television's hottest show,*
$15 million in future deals, and they're starring in a Big Summer
Movie.™ But is Hollywood about to give them an anal probe?

BY MICHaEL ANGELi   PHOTOGRaPH BY DaN WiNTERS

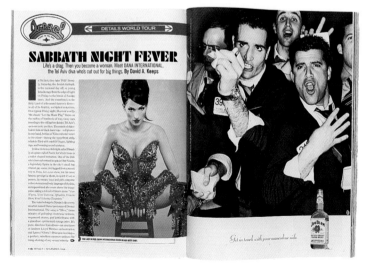

To mark the reopening of the Finnish Museum of Photography, in January 1999, Caryn Faure Walker introduces work by three emerging Finnish installation photographers who aspire to be international while staying rooted in the local

DURING THE EARLY 1980s, Asko Mäkelä, Director of the Finnish Museum of Photography in Helsinki, saw a change in Finnish photography. Cheap travel permitted artists and curators wider access to the art of other Europeans. The introduction of colour eased aside black-and-white documentary and conceptual art and video became influential. Finnish photographers accessed the world's first information highway to research the new work they were encountering.

Mäkelä is proud of how this has helped the Finns intensify their commitment to a broad definition of photography. His museum, founded in 1969, has, as a result, been in a process of renovation and enlargement. When it reopens in January, to anticipated increased audiences, it will have: a major collection of negatives and photographic works, a yearly acquisitions budget, a database and library and an exhibition space of some 800 square meters for permanent and temporary exhibitions. In short, it will provide a sounding board for the young photographers whose work is described in this article. Each in his or her thirties, all went through the University of Industrial Arts, Helsinki in the early 1990s, at a time when Finland was itself confidently emerging from isolation. Their work carries this special sense. Critically aware of international art and media culture, it is rooted equally in the local and the global, or to use a recently invented adjective, the 'glocal'.

Ola Kolehmainen, Marjaana Kella and Jyrki Parantainen register in their work Finland's geography (cities and emptiness) and its climate: a short season of long warm days of light and many months of cold, darkness. They are keenly aware that Finland has been an occupied territory which has had to make its identity from scratch. They reject, however, earlier tendencies to paper over the cracks of ethnic difference necessitated by the rapid invention of history. [1] In an effort to excavate the past, the neighbouring Baltic States and the former Soviet Union have become of interest, particularly to Kolehmainen and Parantainen. The three rigorously work the material of this new milieu along the lines of idea-driven, conceptual art. Each generates projects over two to five years, a rigour also seen in the technical sophistication of image production.

If tension between extremes is a signifier of being Finnish, in these photographic installations, then their stylistic traces come from American minimalist influences in the form of object sculpture's obdurate, physical presence. Light in the work is a signifier of an older, European history of alchemy and also a more recent phenomenological approach to perception. Their photographs demand active watchfulness, and a slowed tangible measurement. Visual pleasure comes via the clarity of detail, gloss and high colour (borrowed from advertising or

FINLAND'S NEW INSTALLATION PHOTOGRAPHY

Left: Jyrki Parantainen.
detail from 25.2.1997.
Helsinki, Finland
Opposite: 23.6.1996.
Haapsalu, Estonia (detail)
Following two spreads:
24.5.1998. Helsinki,
Finland (installation view).
24.5.1998. Helsinki.
Finland (detail)

CC
18

Creative Camera *(UK, Issue 355, 1999) 210 x 280mm*

Fonts based on everyday typography – car number plates, stencils, dot matrices – are used to try and draw attention away from the design and let the photography dominate. Yet the classical structure to the type confirms the page is very designed. The regular set of parts – headline, standfirst and body text – are all featured but not in the normal, expected sequence. Because their hierarchical relationship remains clear, the design can be easily understood.

Designer Phil Bicker

by Raul A. Barreneche

Iceland's new Supreme Court by Studio Granda reflects
the country's politically open and geologically charged character.

ARCTIC JUSTICE

INNER SPACE

by Raul A. Barreneche

Des Moines-based architect Herbert Lewis
Kruse Blunck transforms an ordinary
warehouse into a compelling workplace
focused on industry and light.

GRAVITATIONAL PULL

INVISIBLY ANCHORED MASSES AND COMPLEX PLAYS OF LIGHT FILL THE BUILDINGS BY SPANISH ARCHITECT JUAN NAVARRO BALDEWEG.

Juan Navarro Baldeweg was already established as one of Spain's finest painters when he achieved recognition as one of its most talented architects. In 1982, Navarro Baldeweg completed his first building, the Rain House, a project that brought him international acclaim. The modest dwelling, built for his brother, is located near Santander on Spain's rainy northern coast, where the architect was born in 1939. Critics and architects were instantly enamored by the building's diminutive volume, tautly wrapped in stone and zinc panels and windows that fold over the edge of the roof to keep occupants always aware of the frequent rainfall outside.

In the 15 years since the completion of the Rain House, Navarro Baldeweg has bested some of his country's leading architects in competitions for public buildings throughout Spain. These elegant structures, all of exquisite composition and refinement, include a social center (1988) and a library (1992) in Madrid; a hydrology museum in Murcia (1988); a ravishing but unbuilt congress center for Cadiz (1988); a conference center in Salamanca (1992); and regional government offices in Merida (1995). Over the past five years, the Madrid architect has also won invited competitions in other European countries, including an entertainment center in Blois, France (1991), and a conference center in Salzburg, Austria (1992). Navarro Baldeweg currently teaches full-time at Madrid University, where he earned a Ph.D. in architecture in 1969.

Spanish painter and architect Juan Navarro Baldeweg distills regional building traditions into Modern forms. He applied local stone and stucco to the planar volumes of the Mahon courthouse (facing page).

He has also held visiting professorships in the United States at the University of Pennsylvania, Yale, and Princeton—where his latest building, an addition to the Woolworth Center for Music, was completed last month. Sensitive and poetic, the 58-year-old architect now runs a quiet, eight-person office in El Viso, a leafy, residential section of Madrid, near the home of his better-known contemporary, José Rafael Moneo.

Navarro Baldeweg's colorful, abstract paintings and serene buildings make manifest the presence of such ambient natural phenomena as gravity, light, rain, and wind. For all the beauty of his works, the architect's primary goal is to draw attention away from the physical attributes of his buildings and make viewers open up to the imagined or actual perceptions of nature.

His buildings respond so sensitively to contexts with local materials and traditional massing as to seem an inevitable part of them. Yet each building is also part of a series that reworks an imposed formal device to exploit apparently mutual contradictions. For instance, the heavy, concrete dome of the Salamanca Congress Center's auditorium seemingly floats on the light that floods down and around it. Gravity seems suspended, bringing it to heightened attention, while light becomes so tangible as to seemingly buoy up the massive dome. Like many of his works, the building provokes a similarly contrary response of simultaneous exuberance and hushed sobriety.

In his most recent projects, Navarro Baldeweg is exploring new expressive formal devices, including steel-and-concrete structural frames that form canopies of skylights in the newly completed Villanueva de la Cañada cultural center (pages 114-117), two-directional brise-soleils, as in the government center in Merida, and angularly fragmented, collagist compositions as in the Princeton music school addition (page 112). Their most distinctive features are elements that admit and modulate light from opposite directions.

Navarro Baldeweg is a dreamer who both yearns and yet can barely stand to bring his exquisite works into the real world, where they might be defiled by meddling bureaucrats and insensitive users. Whatever forms he explores—even familiar elements such as domes and walls of stone or brick—his buildings still convey a sense of abstractness, even lightness verging on immateriality. This magic, nearly tangible light and atmosphere is characteristic of what the architect always seeks through the extreme formal refinement of his work. "I want to create an equilibrium where strength of geometry mitigates against, and detaches from us, the weightiness of material," Navarro Baldeweg asserts. "With formal perfection, architecture becomes more invisible and less oppressive, so that one feels free to be fully oneself."

URBAN CONSTRUCT

By Aaron Betsky

Eric Owen Moss and developers Frederick and Laurie Smith continue their piece-by-piece rebuilding of Culver City with a headquarters for an electronic graphics company.

ART INTO ARCHITECTURE

by Joseph Giovannini

Frank Gehry's raw, expressive buildings disturbed the prevailing architectural ethos in the early 1970s by introducing the irrational into a profession dominated by the rational. Subsequent projects confirm the artist's sculptural approach to architectural design, and reveal the influence of the many years he has spent in the company of artists.

Nixon was President, the design material of choice for corporate America was chrome, and Frank Gehry was running a conventional architectural practice. Trained in the conservative architecture school at the University of Southern California and in the detail-oriented Los Angeles firm Gruen Associates, where he worked from 1954 to 1955 and again from 1957 to 1960, Gehry seemed destined to run an upper-middle-quality office, but for his inspired flaw. As a USC student, he switched from art to architecture, and the lateral slide would typify his entire career: while he maintained a practice consonant with the expectations of his time and place, he led a double life, spending time with the iconoclastic artists of Venice Beach who were devising new ways of interpreting space, light, and materiality. At his 1969 show in the Riko Mizuno Gallery, painter Ed Moses took a buzz saw to the roof and opened an oculus to the sky, exposing the ends of the rafters. To materialize light and to paint the air, the artist—working with assistant James Turrell—stood on a ladder and threw rice dust high into the space.

Artists like Larry Bell, Billy Al Bengston, Tony Berlant, Robert Irwin, Moses, and Doug Wheeler invented the conversation Gehry was really listening to, and what he heard differed from what he had learned at USC and Gruen. The Venice artists, most associated with the Ferus Gallery, were pursuing two artistic initiatives. They brought art off the pedestal, out of the frame, and off the wall, utilizing space and light as its subject matter; and they were performing half-serious, half-madcap, quasi-architectural interventions in their own studios, building impromptu moments. Moses, for example, sandwiched wood studs between panes of glass in his bathroom, and Bell created a parallelogrammatic room with all walls leaning toward the beach. Bengston continuously rebuilt his studio, testing out recycled aircraft materials. The efforts specially chosen sites had a relationship to the raw, ongoing, never-finished, at-home construction performances that were undertaken by artists simply because they wanted to: it was a way to talk both to each other and to their art.

It is hard to remember how strictly codified the practice of architecture then was, but design by many highly regarded firms was academically formulaic. The plans by The Architects Collaborative (Walter Gropius's successor firm in Cambridge, Massachusetts) for the national headquarters of the American Institute of Architects in Washington, D.C., built in 1970, generally embodied the prevailing ethos and rules: exposed structure, defined circulation, the materiality of materials, all in the name of simplicity. From the point of view of architectural professionalism, Gehry indulged in deviant behavior when he brought the artists' experiments into his designs. In this new lexicon, materials need not be noble, they could be broken and even chaotic. Collage constituted fair compositional technique. Just as Robert Rauschenberg made artworks out of discarded objects he found in his forays into the trash heaps of

Santa Monica Place
1980

Gehry house,
Santa Monica
1978 renovation

---

model from one project and place it on another, and if it worked, it stayed. A kick to a façade might improve it. Gehry increasingly designed by eye and instinct rather than cerebration. Or, put another way, he no longer conceived buildings on paper with pencil, but designed structures with his hand. Like artists who had come off the wall, he came off the drawing board: hand-built models in their obvious and splendid three-dimensionality yielded far richer form, space, materiality, and light. Though Gehry would deny it—"I'm not an artist, I'm an architect," he insisted—he designed by sculpting. He was interested in presence.

Gehry's great contribution to the field was to break through the art/architecture barrier. Though architects like Philip Johnson and I. M. Pei had long collected art, they rarely let art influence their design. The fields were separate. Gehry crossed the disciplines just as artists were already doing. Artists in many ways, at least Gehry's friends, were more adventurous than the architects, and Gehry was the first to cross-pollinate in the opposite direction. Like all the artists in Venice, he was loathe to theorize about his work, but a small opus—the Ron Davis house in Malibu (1972) and the Spiller duplex in Venice (1980)—was beginning to constitute a non-verbal thesis that would dislocate the field.

The great break-out building was, of course, the 1978 design for his own house on Washington Boulevard in Santa Monica, where he orchestrated corrugated metal, chain-link scrims, light paintings, and Gordon Matta-Clark-like deconstructions into an anti-symphonic non-whole that opened a new chapter in American architectural history. He treated his old Dutch Colonial house as an objet trouvé, wrapping the exterior with a kitchen that curators would call an installation. The result was a cross between an artist's studio and site-specific sculpture. The neighbors objected because it challenged the assumed suburban contract. And many of the artists were disturbed because they saw someone take their ideas even farther.

Gehry's great advantage over artists was that he was, indeed, an architect, and the smallest of his commissions, even a house addition, amounted to an installation bigger than what most artists could or would aspire to short of Land art. The larger venue could simultaneously support a large number of moves. Gehry's house was a summary piece for a movement, biographical for as synopsis of the many ideas coursing through studios in the 1970s, and

The art ideas Gehry brought into architecture irreverently challenged a whole value system consolidated during decades of Modernism.

autobiographical, as it summarized what fascinated him during his long apprenticeship.

Looking at art for architectural inspiration became a pattern, and as Gehry's reputation grew, his terrain of inspiration widened. For the Winton guest house (1987)—a still-life of disparate variously clad forms—Giorgio Morandi was an obvious source. His collaboration with Claes Oldenburg and Coosje van Bruggen resulted in a giant pair of binoculars as a garage entry and façade to the Chiat/Day office building in Venice (1991). The power of the work was in Gehry's interpretative ability to transform the inspiration into an architectural equivalent.

Beyond the specific influence—and beyond the anxiety of that influence—lay a changed attitude. The most profound lesson learned from artists, whether in California or New York, was that architects can also be free to follow their curiosity and instinct—that they can catch themselves in a moment of fascination and pursue architecture, and build the fascination.

Equipped with this attitude, Gehry has gradually become independent of the imaginations that were

his original inspiration. The instrument by which he achieved his independence was the fish. Gehry likes to tell the story of how his grandmother kept a carp in the bathtub of their family home in Toronto to make gefilte fish. The more direct inspiration for his long dalliance with the fish probably grew out of an eagle he drew atop his entry to the mock rerun of the Chicago Tribune competition, held in the early 1980s. The eagle migrated to a design for a house in Bel-Air, where he proposed a phalanx of animal sentries along the driveway, with an eagle near a fish. The fish became a stand-in figure in projects when the real design eluded Gehry, and then it became a why-not? figure—why not actually build a fish? He designed walk-in fish for museum installations and designed fish lamps, followed by the Fishdance restaurant in Kobe, Japan (1987). Related to the piscine shapes were his crocodile and octopus lamps at Rebecca's restaurant in Venice (1985), and his fantasy plan for a fish tower supporting half of a Manhattan suspension bridge (1981); the other half was to be held up by a metal parallelepiped conceived by Serra. The Gehry fish and Serra abstraction each anchored opposite ends of the suspension cable.

Gehry, who can ruminate on a form for decades, dwelled on the fish, and it yielded unexpected results. He observed at least three things. The first was that when the head and tail are removed, the figure quickly becomes abstract: the fish holding up its end of the Manhattan suspension bridge, beheaded and un-tailed, starts becoming as abstract as Serra's pylon at the other end. The second observation was that a fish structure—glimpsed from the corner of the eye—seems to move, like a many-armed Shiva. That is, there is life in a form that curves through space, especially at the end of a curve where it flips. Thirdly, Gehry learned that the computer is indispensable for building a fish's forms—compound curves are among architecture's most intractibly difficult shapes.

The pursuit of fish, which for years seemed merely an amusing indulgence, yielded surprising results at Gehry's Vitra.

Winton guest house,
Wayzata, Minnesota
1987

Fishdance restaurant,
Kobe, Japan
1987

Chiat/Day office
building, Venice,
California
1991

American Center, Paris
1994

Nationale-Nederlanden
building, Prague
1996

Catia rendering of the
Guggenheim Museum
Bilbao's atrium

International Furniture Museum (1989), across the border from Basel, where compound curves form a constantly evolving shape that motivates visitors to walk around the building: the forms are in ever-changing relationships to themselves, curves playing off curves. From the point of view of Gehry's development, the building signaled that he had at last achieved an independence from insights borrowed from his artist mentors. He understood the spirit behind their observations and ten years after the house, made his own independent breakthrough. Architects are said to mature late; Gehry was 60 years old. For inspiration, he now was looking at the sails of magnificent galleons, and at the folds in the drapes of medieval marble sculpture. Anything was fair game.

In their independence from the academy and from the visual rationalities of architecture—the most expensive and therefore most rationalized of the arts—Gehry's buildings embody an especially American attitude that perhaps represents the first significant original architectural idea to land on European shores since Frank Lloyd Wright's Wasmuth portfolio, a German publication of his Oak Park work, which had a great impact on European architecture. The spirit that Gehry's work in Europe incarnates—first Vitra, then the American Center in Paris (1994), the Nationale-Nederlanden building (nicknamed the Fred and Ginger tower) in Prague (1996), and the Guggenheim in Bilbao—is American in its wildness. Gehry was exporting raw, generous, Western vitality to the old world.

Consider his design for the Guggenheim Museum Bilbao. The tough industrial cityscape of this Basque capital requires a building that can stand up to the context, and the mandate of the museum itself stipulated an architecture able to broadcast its presence and establish a wide sphere of influence. The cultural ecology of Europe required no less than a Sydney Opera House for Bilbao: in a unified

The cultural ecology of Europe required for Bilbao: in a unified Europe where nations advance, stellar buildings will help no less than a Sydney Opera House are receding in importance as cities define the cultural pecking order.

Europe where nations are receding in importance as cities advance, stellar buildings will help define the cultural pecking order. Bilbao leaders want their city to be no less than the capital of the Atlantic seaboard in Europe's newly reconfigured geocultural map, and the Gehry building, combined with the Guggenheim collection, will help promote that claim. Of all museums, the Guggenheim knows the power of a building to define an institution. Gehry has delivered a building that at least matches the brilliance of Wright's New York Guggenheim vortex, and the inexplicability of its forms will draw thousands of visitors to its mysteries.

The commission for Bilbao occurs at a mature point in his use of the new language of curves. Sited along Bilbao's industrial riverfront, next to a bridge, in the bowl of the city's valley, the building turns and scrolls along the river, bracketing the bridge and its highway and absorbing them into its force field, then coming to a head in a dense, imploding entry where the curved walls turn and surge up into a spray of white water: the movement of the forms gives the building an energy and life just at the edge of tumult. The central organizing space for the vast museum recalls Wright's rotunda and is meant to provoke site-specific artistic responses. At the request of the Guggenheim, Gehry has not sought a neutralized atrium, but one that stands on its own as an architectural work.

The irony of the design is that without looking technological, its artistic imperative required advanced computer technology. Gehry designed the building with sheets of paper that he rolled and taped by hand, much like a sculptor working clay or a first grader cutting-and-pasting. Baroque craftsmen might be able to carve by hand focal moments on a building, but the sum total of long curves Gehry proposed far exceeded the capabilities of conventional construction practice. Gehry had turned to the computer to execute the Fishdance restaurant, and with his design for the Walt Disney Concert Hall in Los Angeles (still unbuilt) and then the Guggenheim, his reliance was complete. Associates in the office located Catia software, used by the French aeronautical firm Dassault to model jets such as the Mirage, to "build" the necessary drawings.

Catia enabled Gehry to digitize points on the edges, intersections, and surfaces of his hand-built models to construct on-screen models that could then be manipulated like animated cartoons. All intersections and edges are located within the computer in a mathematically knowable spatial matrix. Unlike most CAD applications, Catia allowed Gehry dimensional control of complex shapes, and he was therefore able to use the computer not for representational purposes but as part of the construction process. For Disney Hall, this meant that a disk sent to a computer driving cutting tools in a quarry in the south of France could automatically carve out stone without the usual shop drawings. One computer could speak to another. The same program allowed the Italian construction firm Permasteelisa to build with great accuracy and little waste the monumental webbed fish overlooking the Villa Olimpica complex in Barcelona (1992). The computer has enabled Gehry—and the profession—to realize architectural complexities that would have been impractical only a few years ago. It also challenges the assumption of simplicity necessitated by industrial repetition, which has long formed the conceptual basis of architectural Modernism. The computer can handle uniqueness rather than repetition without punishing costs, and in the long run it has the potential of shifting practice to a post-industrial paradigm based on electronics rather than mechanics.

The creativity of artists who do not finally exceed their inspiration eventually tires and expires, but Gehry clearly has sustained a body of work that has emerged with a logic and life of its own. Whatever derivations may have sparked his first break-out designs no longer direct his imagination. In a practice characterized by grasping beyond what he has already reached, Gehry has achieved an originality that not only influences architects but also the artists who were his first inspiration and example. ●

PREVIOUS SPREAD **Architecture** (US, 1997) 270 x 340mm
Four opening spreads that demonstrate the power afforded by digital technology, enabling the headline type to be integrated into the photographs rather than just float on the surface. Full-bleed architectural photography is the ideal vehicle for this process of allowing the visual elements to be combined to emphasize the planes and shapes involved.
Art director J. Abbott Miller

THIS SPREAD **Guggenheim Magazine** (US, 1997) 270 x 340mm
Instead of working to a pre-conceived grid, the type grows from the images, carefully but randomly reflecting the content of the photographs.
Art director J. Abbott Miller

Vogue Homme International Mode *(Italy, Issue 4, Autumn/Winter 1998/99) 228 x 297mm*

Part of a series of mini-features that run at the front of this fashion magazine, these pages are designed to relate through general structure rather than the use of a strict grid or headlining system. This makes it very flexible yet helps the editorial stand apart from the ads. The boldest part of most pages is the picture, but the eye is drawn to the subtle headline and standfirst by the small coloured square at the top of each page.

Art director *Phil Bicker*

The coolest thing about Mash – Oliver Peyton's new and glorified London pizza joint – are the loos. The urinals are a bulge in a wall of distorted mirror which makes your penis look momentarily larger than life. Next door girls get to play voyeur as video screens show simultaneous transmission of what's happening in the boys' room. A sly touch is no-one has bothered to tell the boys they are being filmed. Sitting out front sipping a pint is the wit behind the loos, Murray Partridge a man who calls himself an ideas consultant. That means he comes up with the creative idea (in this case: "What about reflective urinals that make your willy look bigger"), you pay the cash, take the idea and do something with it. A former advertising exec and before that an accountant who was fired for photocopying his bottom ("So, that was a shit idea" admits Murray), he had the consultancy idea four years ago. Since then his ideas have included persuading Lego to use a dysfunctional family as heroes for its new Scala ad campaign, G-shock to make a watch scattered with diamonds and budget airline Easyjet to invest in a major ad/marketing campaign which gets off on its own bargain-basement cheesiness. Partridge is an example of the new breed in service industry – the creative dictator. Spawned by a culture which is cash happy, short on time and craves originality and ideas, the creative dictator is getting rich quick by advising on our every aesthetic decision. They tell us how to dress, how to party, how to be hip, how to sharpen our brand image and how to make urinals sexy. They have positioned themselves at the cutting edge of their subject, be that food, paint, fashion or furniture and in a generation where specialist knowledge is all, we are paying them to download a slice of theirs.

"If you want a divorce go to a lawyer, if you want a sofa fit for a collection come to me," is how French contemporary design consultant Didier Krzentowski sees it. He is the perfect example of the creative dictator – the consummate know-it-all on his subject. An official Expert in Design and Contemporary Art with a "private bulimia for collecting", he is a constant itinerant wandering from the Left Bank to Tokyo via Bilbao to meet artists, furniture designers, see shows, bid at sale rooms and buy. Clients hire him for his taste, his time, his contacts and his ability to short circuit the collecting loop. "Imagine you are someone with a lot of cash and intelligence, either you can spend all the time in the world looking for a sofa," suggests Krzentowski from his apartment littered with 20th century design epics – a vase by Martin Szekely, a book-case by TKTK, "Or you can tell

me the sort of look you had in mind and in ten minutes I can get on the telephone and find the perfect sofa from around the world (itals) and (end itals) explain why you want it in your collection." And here's the heady pull of the creative dictator – you can pay them to "enhance" your taste. "Someone who spends all day looking at stocks and bonds is not necessarily going to be the sort of person who knows how to look at something aesthetically – unless it happens to have a price tag" says a diplomatic David Oliver, paint consultant and owner of chic Chelsea paint shop the Paint Library. "Nor, probably, does he have the time to spend every Saturday looking at pieces of wallpaper, fabric swatches and colour charts." So, someone who spends all day looking at stocks and bonds employs someone like David to tell them which colour to paint their house. For a fee of £75 an hour, he will come round to your place and turn his taste to colour combinations, paint test patches on the walls and tell you what's cool and what is not. "Often they just want a masculine opinion about the flat" says David about his clients, "They've had too much of their mother's advice or their girlfriend's advice and they want another man's viewpoint on

what is going to be sexy and work for them." In a world swimming in product, choices and brands, objective opinions are just what we need. At the Sonia Rykiel boutique in Paris, director and personal shopper Yves Melsen puts together looks and outfits for clients including private visits to Matignon to kit out French prime-minister Lionel Jospin in made-to-measure Rykiel. "Most men come for my objective advice" says Melsen "Also the fact we are specialists, we have an eye, we know the product and we respect the image of our client and the image they would like to communicate." Melsen compares his work to that of a doctor, asking all the right questions then prescribing a sartorial solution which fits both

A selection from David Oliver's Paint Library. For £75 an hour he'll tell what's cool and what is not.

Brooks Brothers tropical

Thomas Beller buys a shirt in Phnom Penh

One of the first things a new visitor to Phnom Penh is likely to notice is how well-dressed most of the men are. Monsoon rains may turn the streets into shallow lakes, the electricity may be erratic, but the men are fairly consistent in their outfit – a pair of slacks and a neat button-down short-sleeved shirt.

The supply of T-shirts I had brought suddenly seemed woefully inadequate, perhaps even disrespectful, and so I set out to buttress my shirt supply. I went straight to the Central Market. I was always greeted with great warmth and enthusiasm at the Central Market, due to a happy coincidence regarding the Khmer language; I am quite tall, a little over six foot five, and my first name is Tom, which is the Khmer word for big. Thus, everywhere that I went, people would call out my name.

It soon became apparent that the fact that I am Tom, so to speak, was of no advantage in the shirt department, as none fitted. I wound my way through the labyrinthine byways of the market with increasing desperation, but it was only when I arrived in the meat section – amidst the dripping livers on hooks, the goose-bumped skin of plucked chickens hanging by twisted necks, the chopped pig hoofs – that I stumbled on the fabric shop of Ms Huon Na Lin.

At the back of Ms Lin's stall was an arrangement of solid-coloured fabrics arranged in a neatly overlapping spread. From 1979 to 1988 this was the prevailing fabric of choice, but then a new fabric arrived called "Spok". The old style was solids, the new was stripes. It was no contest. Now, she explained to me, the stripes reigned supreme. A glance around the market confirmed her statement – stripes abounded. A yellow background with white stripes was the best seller, and I asked for it. She looked me up and down and produced a handsome blue with white stripes. The yellow is for girls, she said. I bought 2.5 metres for five dollars.

She looked me up and down and produced a handsome blue with white stripes. The yellow is for girls, she said

I found the Paris Mode Tailor a block from the market. The proprietor was Ving Chea, a 67-year-old man with sloped shoulders and a row of gleaming gold teeth in the corner of his mouth. He wore a tank-top T-shirt and had a tape-measure draped around his wrinkly neck. His thinning hair rose off the top of his head in disarray, pointing in different directions like the periscopes of a lost fleet of submarines.

I presented Mr Chea with my fabric and then produced a Brooks Brothers Oxford – the one dress shirt I had brought – and asked that he duplicate it. Mr Chea examined the Brooks Brothers product with the hasty assurance of a man who knows shirts.

Mr Chea didn't so much sew a shirt for me as concoct one. I collected it several days later and, ever since, have possessed a shirt of great distinction. It has nearly magical powers – the main trick being that people immediately comment on it favourably. My theory about why is as follows: so much about Phnom Penh was aesthetically strange and unfamiliar to my eyes, it made sense that a shirt made there should leap out at my compatriots in New York as something profoundly, viscerally unusual. Perhaps it was the deep purple, I mused, or the bright white stripes.

One evening I stood wearing the thing at a party. I'd been back in New York for months, but had yet to grow weary of advertising my travels. A fashion enthusiast rubbed the fabric between her fingers, and made approving and appreciative noises on the cut. I was about to launch into another windy and over-proud explanation of the shirt's exotic origins when something caught my eye. For the first time I noticed a small sentence printed on the inside of the fabric. It required a double take to fully apprehend it, and it had a chastening effect. It read: "Made in the USA." 🔵

'Seduction Theory' by Thomas Beller is published in July by Abacus at £9.99

AN

There are sti

Discover the Fr

But the East Europeans had had enough of Carlos by 1985. He needed another refuge. It may have been Vergès who arranged for him to go to Syria, the obvious choice for a man who was *persona non grata* in Iraq. Certainly one former Stasi agent has recently claimed that Vergès and Ramirez met in Damascus in 1986. The Syrians kept him until 1992. By then he had become an embarrassment and was drinking. So they shuffled him on, first to Jordan, then to Khartoum. He was of no further use, except to Pasqua.

The speciality of Charles Pasqua is law and order, and in particular anti-terrorism. In the run-up to the presidential election Pasqua has an important role to play. The favourite candidates for the right-wing ticket are both Gaullists, the prime minister Edouard Balladur and the ex-prime minister and mayor of Paris, Jacques Chirac. Pasqua is a former lieutenant of Chirac and currently the principal lieutenant of Balladur. If Balladur is chosen then Pasqua's role as kingmaker would give him a strong chance of the premiership. If Chirac is chosen it will be because Pasqua has agreed to switch his support. If neither gets it then Pasqua himself has an outside chance. But in order to deploy his maximum influence, Mr Pasqua has to show that he is *en pleine forme*. He has to be seen to be, to use his own phrase, "terrorizing the terrorists".

The abduction and trial of "Carlos the Jackal" is a typical Pasqualian pre-election ploy. In the run up to the last presidential election in 1988 Pasqua mounted a similar production, a paramilitary "anti-terrorist" operation in the French colony of New Caledonia. Unfortunately the whole thing backfired on the eve of the poll, too many people were killed and it turned into another police fiasco. But this time it is happening in Paris, and Pasqua is confident he can keep it under control. Once the DST had located Carlos in Khartoum it was a relatively straightforward question of arranging the terms of the deal. One possible scenario would have been: 1, two Iranian terrorists to Teheran. 2, Iranian oil to Khartoum. 3, Carlos to Paris. The actual terms are unlikely to be revealed but it is known that Jean-Charles Marchiani, Pasqua's veteran roving ambassador in the Middle East, was heavily involved.

Will there be a second bombing campaign, this time to release Ramirez himself? Pasqua clearly thinks not. Carlos seems to have lost his last Arab patron and his network is no longer active. Magdalena Kopp has retired to Venezuela, where she is bringing up the child she had with Ramirez. "There will be no reprisals," says Vergès. "My client is not a gangster. Whatever he did, he did for political reasons. But there is no doubt that he will receive a life sentence. After all, he is a major terrorist, a *chef de bande*." By this phrase Maitre Vergès means that Ramirez, at the end of the road, remains an equal and is entitled to respect. Isn't that rather an unusual description of his client by the defence lawyer? "Why?" replies Vergès. "For him, the word is a badge of honour." It seems that this time Vergès and Pasqua have nothing to negotiate over.

For those who notice the prison van as it plies between La Santé and the Ile de la Cité next month, and who recall the events of September 1986, that will be a relief. ●

CORRESPONDENCE

Geoff Dyer
braces himself for Valentine's Day

Please, please, Mr Postman

The thing about Valentine's Day is that it is a day just like any other. I have no strong feelings about it one way or the other. In the hierarchy of festive days it is no more intrusive than Mother's Day or Father's Day and is a lot better since there is always post on Valentine's Day unless Valentine's Day happens to fall on a Sunday which means that it really is not Valentine's Day at all but a Sunday, which is exactly the same as a bank holiday Monday, which is a post-less day. Normally, though, Valentine's Day does not just

The only kind of post that interests me is the kind that comes in Jiffy bags, containing books or CDs

than the various bank holidays, which are terrible, which are really just Sundays, which, if I could, I would abolish immediately. Since I never work, other people's not working means simply a diminution of service provision. Every day is a Sunday for me so I do not need the state to provide any extra ones. A bank holiday is above all a day when there is no post, so in this respect Valentine's Day is clearly preferable

mean the possibility of post but the possibility of *extra* post, not as much post as you might expect on your birthday but more than usual even though this post, the post that arrives on Valentine's Day, is of no great inter-

est to me, but at least there *is* post, at least there is the *possibility* of post and for this we should be grateful since a bank holiday Monday is above all a day when there is no hope of post, which means that bank holiday Mondays are really bank holiday Sundays. The post that arrives on Valentine's Day is of no interest to me because, aside from cheques, the only kind of post that does interest me is the kind that comes in Jiffy bags, the kind containing books or CDs. Essentially, unless it comes in a Jiffy bag I'm not interested. My ideal Valentine card would be a compliments slip with a CD enclosed, the kind of package, in other words, that I might receive on any other day of the year except a Sunday or a bank holiday Monday…

Which makes me think, as I consider this further, that on balance perhaps I am anti-Valentine's Day because in a sense it *is* like a bank holiday in that what benefits the rest of the population affects me adversely because the general increase in the volume of post in the days preceding Valentine's Day means that there is a chance, a strong possibility in fact, that the post I

'It is not a gangster. r he did, he did for reasons' – Vergès

Esquire OPPOSITE
(UK, July/August 1995)
220 x 300mm

Esquire THIS PAGE
(UK, February 1995)
220 x 300mm
Shapes cut into the columns of text to provide a simple but effective illustration of the content.
Art director
Christophe Gowans

It's a sweltering afternoon in August in an empty civic hall in Wolverhampton. On stage, a guitarist and a singer are performing. It's only a sound check but they're playing for real. Standing at the back of the hall, the cleaner and I have never heard anything quite so beautiful. The Verve are coming back from rock 'n' roll death.

Two years earlier, the band split up amid rumours of mental instability, heavy drug abuse and even heavier egos. At the time, in July 1995, they were reckoned the most exhilarating band in Britain. They, the forerunners of Britpop, precursors of Oasis, were on the very brink. Then nothing — until this summer.

He's not properly famous, but Richard Ashcroft, lead singer and mainspring of The Verve, is preceded by quite a reputation. He has, it's been said, "the eyes of a missionary", a genius tongue, the focus of Kasparov and narcotically good looks, somewhere between Jim Morrison and the Artful Dodger. Both Ashcroft and Nick McCabe, the band's lead guitarist — then and now — come from Wigan; both are 25. Ashcroft is calm for a rock star, albeit an out-of-practice one, but claims to have a chip on his shoulder "big enough for the world to eat". McCabe is a compulsive perfectionist, who rarely says a word. It is probably the tension between them that gives their music its edge. It's also what led to the band's break-up — and might still lead to a turbulent future.

For The Verve, re-formed, are once more on the brink. Last week, their new single, The Drugs Don't Work, went straight to number one in the charts; next week, they are supporting Oasis at Earls Court; and the week after that, their new album comes out. Their on-off career has run in parallel with their friends and allies in Oasis. Four years ago, Oasis supported The Verve on tour. Then, after the split, the Gallaghers stood by Ashcroft during his months in the wilderness. Now, supporting Oasis, they are expected to make a good pairing: Oasis brasher and barnstorming, The Verve emotional and celebratory, but subtler and more sophisticated.

Ashcroft was born the son of a hairdresser and an unemployed builder. He lost his father at the age of 11 to a freak blood clot on the brain. Like other boys who suffer such a loss at a key point in their lives, Ashcroft became a tearaway. He bunked off school (one time, they dredged the canal, not realising he was sunbathing on a nearby hill) and rejected the companionship of most people, including those his own age. "That doesn't mean I hate them or don't want what they want. I think anger is a very valid emotion."

There was never any money around and Ashcroft's relatives seem to have been as disorientated as he was. One memory that haunted his childhood, and haunts him still, was an astronomy lesson from his grandfather: "I just couldn't get over the fact that my grandfather used to show me the stars when I was five years old and told me that space was infinite and that some of those stars might not exist. So, all my life, I've had this incredible feeling that it's crazy. That the world's a little ball of insanity floating in infinity."

It was Ashcroft's stepfather, a maverick schoolteacher with a passion for Rosicrucianism, spiritualism and magic, who helped harness Ashcroft's precocious anarchy and feed his individuality. "He took every bit of conditioning out of my mind. Instinct is the truth. In anything in life, relationships ▶

Two years ago, The Verve were poised to take on the world. Then they split up. And the rest was silence. Until this summer. This month, re-united, the band had a new single go straight to number one. Next week, they're on stage supporting Oasis. They're ready, they say, for a second crack

Once more with feeling

By **Tom Hiney** Photographs by **Sam Piyasena**

28

Going round in circles

To some, crop circles are the work of extra-terrestrials, proof that we are not alone. Others say they are just elaborate, man-made jokes. The truth must be out there somewhere. By **John Vidal**. Pictures by **Neil Drabble**

O n July 7, a massive crop circle appeared overnight in a Wiltshire wheat field. It measured almost a kilometre in circumference and covered several acres. Its edges were elaborately patterned like snowflakes, it was surrounded by hundreds of smaller circles, and its interior was swept to the ground in different directions. From the air, the circle shimmered and glistened like a cut stone. Closer inspection showed that its design was based on complex geometry and progressions of numbers, called "fractals", and that wheat had been laid in up to four layers, sometimes in a dense weave.

There was much excitement at the size and quality of the formation. Ten days after its discovery, 170 people filed into its centre from the small Wiltshire village of Alton Barnes. It was the climax of a crop-circle conference, and the group was led in by Ron Bearcloud Berry, a native American seer and artist from the Odeepe tribe of Arizona. They all held hands and formed a great human circle. As the sun dipped over nearby Silbury Hill and a landscape that features more pagan monuments per square mile than anywhere else in Britain, Bearcloud took an eagle feather and his sacred stones, lit sage, sang a heartsong and drummed. Moving from person to person, he invited everyone to celebrate the "Star

Merry-go-round: Despite the claims to the contrary, believers (main picture) cannot conceive that crop circles could have been made by man

Nations" — the "unknown peoples of the universe", who, he believed, had sent this circle as a loving sign. He asked those present — they included philosophers, hippies, tourists, academics, scientists, new agers, healers, sceptics, ufologists, students and children — to think fine thoughts and then disperse them to the winds.

Many of the assembly were, like Bearcloud, circle "believers". They were convinced that the crop formation they were standing in could not have been made by humans. Some thought it full of meaning and cosmic significance; others saw it as a warning about the late-20th-century human condition. Few of them realised they were being watched — 50 metres away loitered three dark figures.

There was a frisson as word spread that these spectres had been recognised as people who claimed to make circles like the one the believers were standing in, and were considered by many of those present to be malicious liars, cheats and tricksters. The three men were asked to leave. As they retreated, and to the delight of those who believe in cosmic coincidence, three great, black birds passed overhead in formation.

It's all a long way from 1992, when two genial artists in their sixties, Doug Bower and Dave Chorley, went on television to claim that they were responsible for all the simple circles, dice spots, pendulums, crescent moons and whirlpool shapes that had been mysteriously appearing in English fields since the mid-Seventies. They then showed how they did it, with a garden roller and ropes. This was followed by a Guardian-sponsored competition, which brought together 12 groups of would-be hoaxers: asked to copy a random pattern of formations to test their skills, the students, engineers and others who took part conclusively showed that anyone with a bit of practical intelligence could, in just a few hours, make a fair replica of any of the simple shapes that had appeared in the fields using just ropes, hula-hoops, boards and ladders. The lovely, harmless, entertaining mystery, it seemed, was over. End of story.

Except that it wasn't. In the past six years, similar formations have appeared in ever greater numbers all around the world, and their scale, complexity and quality has developed massively. Some have straggled for almost a mile, and others measured 100 metres across. Today's makers have moved on to planetary maps, mandalas, pentagrams, vortices, DNA structures, mazes and labyrinths, double helixes, mystical "trees of life", spinning wheels, formations that look like webs and knots, or snowflakes, computer-generated fractals and complex designs derived from chaos theory. Almost unnoticed, the fields of southern England have been turned into a bizarre canvas of anonymous land art.

Moreover, when deconstructed, the most elaborate of these formations are based on a "sacred" geometry known to the ancients, and obey strict mathematical proportions and complex numerology. Some of them defy immediate attempts to work out how they are made. From the ground, the flattened crops seem to flow like water across the formations. From the air, from where they are often best seen, they look as if they have just dropped softly into the fields.

More than 5,000 such formations have appeared in more than 40 countries, yet no one has ever been caught making the most complex ones, and very few of them have ever been claimed as the work of a hoaxer. Southern England, notably Wiltshire, is the accepted crop circle capital of the world, and the county tourist department busily ▶

The Guardian Weekend *(UK, 1998) 290 x 370mm*
Originally designed for journalists rather than designers to put together, this newspaper supplement is very stripped down and simple. As well as the usual celebrity interviews, it carries stories about cancer and child abuse so it was hard to create a single design personality: instead it has a non-personality, allowing the pictures and words be noticed rather than the design.
Art director Mark Porter

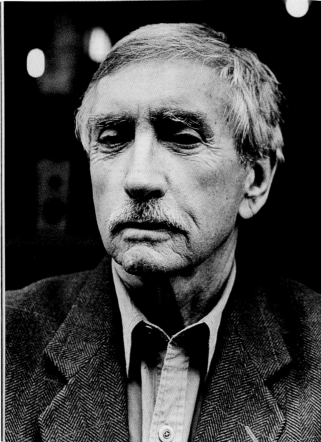

Written by Steven Drukman
Photographed by Richard Dunkley

Didn't he write *Who's Afraid of Virginia Woolf?* Haven't heard from him in a while?
Well, gentle theatergoer, take note: America's greatest living neglected playwright is back.

Edward Albee's Second Act

When all the critics were gushing over *Three Tall Women*, the 1994 play that would earn Edward Albee his third Pulitzer Prize, it seemed like something was amiss—not least of all to Mr. Albee. To this éminence grise of American drama, unanimous critical praise must seem straight out of theater of the absurd. Since the U.S. premiere of *The Zoo Story* in 1960, Albee has been the target of the slings and arrows of outrageous criticism from every direction. The *New York Post* anointed him "the new Eugene O'Neill," while *The New York Times* dismissed *The Zoo Story* as "conventional melodrama." Suspicious critics even detected (in Jerry's throwing himself on Peter's knife) "an unsuccessful homosexual pass."

Which brings us to *Who's Afraid of Virginia Woolf?*, Albee's 1962 hit, later adapted into the 1966 film by Mike Nichols that starred Elizabeth Taylor in an unforgettable turn as Martha, the ice-

chomping, braying faculty wife. Critics like *The New York Times'* Stanley Kauffmann attacked the "disguised homosexual influence" in plays like *Virginia Woolf* because Albee had the temerity to fashion heterosexuals like George and Martha into a "distortion of marriage and femininity." In the Stone Age before Stonewall, it was not only acceptable but laudable to attack gay playwrights—and young Edward Albee became the favored whipping boy.

All this could make a guy pretty cranky, no matter how thick his skin has become after 40 years in the theater. Albee certainly has a reputation: "Prickly," "grim," and "frosty" were the milder adjectives people threw my way to steel me for our interview. I can only report that when I visited Albee in Montauk, New York, where he has a home by the sea with his lover, artist Jonathan

85

STATE OF THE UNION

THE GLOBAL ECONOMY, THE CLINTON SEX SCANDAL, THOSE ANNOYING EX-GAY ADS—IT'S THE LAST MIDTERM ELECTION BEFORE THE CLOSE OF THE CENTURY, AND 'OUT' ASKED SOME MOVERS AND SHAKERS TO FORECAST THE MOST SIGNIFICANT CHALLENGES WE FACE AS WE VOTE THIS NOVEMBER.

Like so many communities—that's community with a capital C—ours is often mired in its own political concerns and petty squabbles. But during the past weeks of economic swerving and months of presidential waffling and weaving, one truth has held fast: National politics—or more correctly the politics that informs our national identity—affects our lives profoundly. Clearly, big-picture politics shapes us, but it is also our right (dare we say duty?) to shape it, not only as gay men and lesbians of different races, classes, and political persuasions but also as workers, consumers, parents, and, ultimately, citizens.

Increasingly, *fragile* is used by politicians and economists to describe the various events peppering our morning and evening news. Business confidence is fragile. Russia's economy and its government are in a delicate state, to put it mildly. The Asian and Latin markets are wilting, and Japan, our partner in global marketing, seems unable (or unwilling) to do the things necessary to spruce them up. And, of course, there's the Clinton presidency, which is exhibiting more than a bit of ethical fatigue.

Each day brings a revised version of the political-economic story. Often it's a tale more disheartening, or at least more confusing, one than the previous day's.

And what that story will be as we head to the voting booths—because vote we must—is indeed uncertain. Will the Republicans, thanks to the Monica-Bill-and-Ken show, not only maintain control of the Senate but also increase their majority to the point

where they are filibuster-proof? Will a bearish market further embolden hawkish attacks not only on the lesbian, gay, bisexual, and transgender community but also on the poor and people with HIV? And what about justice? Will the religious Right be allowed to craft America's political agenda?

We asked some of the politically and philosophically active among us to share their most pressing concerns as we head into this November's election. Needless to say, our interviewees often found it difficult to hew to one issue, when so many are vitally intertwined. And though they did not all agree, even the most combative among them avoided internecine bickering to address the urgency of grander themes.

THE WASHINGTON CONFIDENCE GAME
"As far as I'm concerned, the biggest issue is restoring the confidence of the American people in our political process. We're in a period when people are becoming increasingly cynical about the government. Both political parties seem to have been corrupted by big money, and there is an increasing lack of ideological difference between the two. And because the country is so large, every attempt to establish a third party in the United States has failed; there really is a lack of meaningful political debate. Citizens in general, particularly young people, feel that 'Washington is obsessed with power politics, with turf wars and the personal vanity of ambitious politicians. The people's interests seem very quickly forgotten by politicians once they arrive in Washington. The political process is stuck, stagnant, in a stalemate on every

74

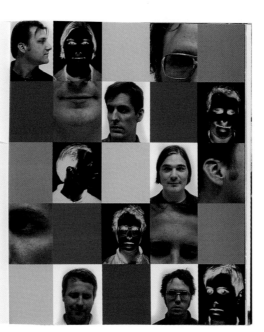

Out (US, November 1998) 205 x 265mm
Creative director Dan Lori

Flaunt (US, Issue 5, June/July 1999) 230 x 275mm
Art directors Eric Roinestad and Jim Turner

Two American magazines that have a minimalist look. When launched in the eighties, *Out* had a very American feel which was recently replaced by this approach (OPPOSITE) featuring subtle sans serif type and large areas of white space. *Flaunt* shares a minimalist typographic approach but combines this with the use of half-size pages, an example of which is shown. The half-page bearing the headline 'Pavement' turns to reveal an interview with the band and covers up the interview with the Beta Band.

☐ ANDREW GROVES

IN ANDREW GROVES' PRESS BIOGRAPHY, LOVINGLY PREPARED AS IT IS (BY A TOP PR COMPANY, OF COURSE) THERE ARE SOME SIGNIFICANT GAPS AMONGST THE TALES OF HIS TRAVELS WITH CARNIVALS, STINTS AS A COSTUMIER AT THE ROYAL SHAKESPEARE COMPANY NATIONAL THEATRE AND MAXIMUM HEADLINE GRABBERY AT SAINT MARTINS.

For instance his former (late 80s/early 90s) incarnation as Jimmy Jumble, legendary designer of preposterous items to wear in discotheques, and stalwart of Sign Of The Times' shops and themed parties.

"What I'm doing now is completely different. That was a difficult market - you could never do any tailoring or use expensive fabrics. I started making clothes and it just sort of happened that they ended up in Sign Of The Times. From what I remember, it was mostly club kids - going out a lot, making stuff, selling it - but no-one taking it very seriously. Though I think what happened, then was important; there were some really interesting things going on - but it's hard to run that type of thing as a business."

Jumble classics included a dress with fake nipples stuck on, a dress made entirely of safety pins (obviously admired by Galliano, a regular in the store, who later did his own 'version') and, best of all, a dress with a lurid print of the human digestive system upon it - which made a delicate fashion editor-type violently sick all over her desk, poor darling.

Alas, it wasn't long before the High Streets became awash with a decidedly more watered-down sort of kitsch. Hence, Jimmy turned back into Andrew and went to do a 'proper' Fashion MA at Saint Martins - as had his former (pre-stardom) boyfriend, Alexander McQueen. Any bitchy beans to spill?

"No, I don't talk about that at all," he hurrumphs, before lighting a ciggie. Saint Martins, then.

"I only went to college to get to do the final show in Fashion Week... I just used to go in once a week. Nobody could cut properly there, so I'd just sit in the office and slag all the other students off. The rest of the time I was working in Regulations - the sex shop... just freaks every day. There were these two guys that used to give each other saline injections to make their balls bigger (as you do) and we'd be making sleeping bags to order for leather people - fitting these fat old blokes into them (laughs). And they were always trying it on in the changing rooms - urgh!"

The aforementioned final collection, Ordinary Madness, was unveiled in February 1997 and comprised impressively tailored women's garments adorned with six inch nails, earning him a distinction, front page coverage in the UK's Daily Rags and gushing recognition as The Next Big Thing in American Vogue. Needless to say, heaps of Hot Fashion Action happened since, much of which was not aided by the quivering British Fashion Council - too scared of his work - so they say - to include him on the official Fashion Week schedules for his subsequent shows - Status and Ourselves Alone. Undeterred, he raised the money himself and found alternative venues (a derelict bus depot in Victoria and the catacombs of Chalk Farm stables). The creaky old BFC were forced to dine on humble pie, because they were easily the most spectacular shows and all the bigwigs buggered off from the schedule to see them, anyway. Status was "all about" disease, with clothes seemingly rotting away as the show proceeded, before a model released a swarm of flies from under her jacket (2,000 in all, specially purchased for £600 from "The people who supplied Damien Hirst"). This caused an erm, bit of a buzz.

"I went to Paris about three weeks ago for an interview with this big couture house (refuses to reveal which one). I didn't really want the job, but I thought it'd be a laugh 'cos all expenses were paid and maybe I'd get to nick some clothes for Trixie (the trannie whose Battersea High Rise living room Andrew rather tragically sleeps in... on a mattress in the corner). The woman who's the head of the couture house said 'The one thing I know about you is you made one of our most prestigious journalists sit in a room full of flies.' She was so put out by it!" sniggers Groves. Yet they still wanted him... badly.

"I only want to do something like that if they let you do what you want," he continues, "but they just wanted to buy into me without understanding what I do. They asked me what I thought of them, so I told them. I said, 'Your catwalk presentation is shit, and the clothes are so old-fashioned. You used to be at the cutting edge, now you've got no idea what's really going on. The French think they're really IT... I just do what I do and if people don't like it - tough."

Similarly wholehearted was the show for 'Ourselves Alone', described in the press blurb as 'A sensitive embrace of the contemporary, still volatile, dispute between Protestant and Catholic.' (The Orange telephone people nearly sponsored it - and in the light of The Orangemen sagas of late, are probably extremely glad they didn't.) There were burnt taffeta fabrics, very dropped Victorian silhouettes, 'Hardcore Motherfucker/Broken English' soundtracks and fire-real flames, no less. (An attendee remarks: "It was scary - the model was on fire and you didn't know if it had gone wrong or was meant to be like that.")

"If you're putting £30,000 into a show, you want it to be something that you wouldn't normally see, and you want to get a reaction. What's the point of having a show unless you're getting a reaction?"

A question chintzy Chelsea designer Bella Freud may have (reluctantly) asked herself. Having coughed up lots of lolly for her inclusion 'on schedule', it must have been frightfully galling to watch one's potential audience scamper to Groves' thrill-athon.

"Apparently, before the show she is still going 'Oh, I'm not worried about him!'" he cackles, "I think she still thinks it's the eighties!"

(Groves is confirmed to be 'on schedule' at the next Fashion Week, and will be debuting his menswear collection, too).

As you may have guessed by now, it ain't all chummy-chummy Happy Families in this biz. With the exception of Comme des Garçons, Martin Margiela and Gaultier, Andrew has little encouragement for his fellow frocksmiths. "Vivienne Westwood?" (adopts mock Lancashire accent) "Ooh I do believe you can create modern couture on a low thread overlock... she's like... crap! Gucci? Just clothes for footballers with too much money. That Jeremy Scott (brattish US designer with parodic mullet hair, indulgent parents and Izzy Blow as a mentor)... he's a New York club kid trying too hard. You can see through the presentation of it and there's nothing behind it - no new ideas or interesting cutting - it's crap. Matthew Williamson? Crap and nothing-ish!"

So what does Andrew think of being hailed by all 'n' sundry as the Controversial/BadBoy/EnfantTerrible/Etc of dizzy Dame Fashion?

"Well, it's only 'cos everyone else is so shit and lame, isn't it?"

ANDREW GROVES' DESIGNS ARE STOCKED IN PELLICANO (LONDON) AND UNITED ARROWS (JAPAN - WHERE HE'S VERY VERY POPULAR INDEED).

JAMES ANDERSON

sleazenation

☐ DIANAS GRAVE AND THE ALTHORP EXPERIENCE

WHAT HAVE MICHAEL FLATELEY, DARREN DAY, JOE LONGTHORNE, CELINE DION, NOEL EDMONDS MICHAEL BOLTON AND NEW TWIT ON THE BLOCK JANE MACDONALD ALL GOT IN COMMON WITH THE UK'S MOST RECENTLY APPOINTED TOURIST ATTRACTION? YES, THEY ALL ATTRACT THAT INVISIBLE MAJORITY WE SOMETIMES REFER TO AS JOE PUBLIC', THE 'STATUS QUO' OR EVEN THE NATION.

And as tourist attractions go this has got to be the weirdest yet. The freak show which has sold out for this year and is attracting two-and-a-half thousand people a day at approximately £9.50 a pop is the burial ground of Princess Diana, Queen of Hearts at Althorp in Northampton.

Naturally Sleaze Nation decided to take a look and find out what The Diana Bemusement Arcade had to offer.

All we knew was that it was in Northampton somewhere off Junction 16a off the M1 and that we should follow signs for Little Brington near Whilton cum Lower Harlestone. Fine? A piece of piss. Descending into a surreal world of pseudo-thatched cottages and cake shops we stumbled rather uninvited (completely in fact as we had no tickets) into the Althorp Experience and entered the designated parking area with no resistance.

It was like Tribal Gathering without ticket touts, mud and people jamming flyers under your windscreen. This was all hampers, tupperware and thermos flasks. It was a Ford Mondeo Rover 600 Renault Espace Robinson's Barley Water sponsored Day Out and travel rugs were compulsory. Our supreme bag of an entrance shall for legal reasons remain a secret but for any joggers out there who fancy their chances here's our tip - don't tell them you're from the press. The first impression as you enter the courtyard is of an air of detached reality. It's not a sombre respectful atmosphere, it's more reminiscent of George A. Romero's Return of the Living Dead. In the scene where two heroes are discussing why the zombies are wandering aimlessly around a shopping centre. Their suitably enigmatic conclusion is 'They come here, but they don't know why!' As far as I can work out people are basically just gawping at each other and wondering what the fuck to do.

A diversion occurs. People shuffle over to an enclosed garden area where two of Earl Spencers' spaniel have been let out to play. It's strictly not a photo opportunity. We are duly warned by a Paparazzi-phobic shade wearing security git who thinks he's in the FBI to 'Not even think about it.' We do a swift one, remembering that we must maintain our undercover status. Entry into the house itself is greeted with customary strict regulatory notices; No Cameras, No Food, No Smoking.

Avoiding a body search from the walkie-talkied bodywarmer-wearing security Sweeny and I gain access. It's the usual stately home nonsense with as little space as possible in which to practice shuffling along the ripped off gangways. The volume of inane banter is now multiplied by the acoustics of the great rooms. Daft questions are rattled off to the mortified staff on hand, obviously only present to make sure nobody nicks anything. Having seen how the other 'art' live (hundred seat dining rooms, posh uncomfortable looking chairs, elaborate non-MFI cabinets, large paintings of the Spencer's privileged past and their too close for comfort relations) we shuffle out again, momentarily pausing to ask why there was a game of Twister in the library.

"Something to do with the family business," mutters one of the 'off-line' attendants who seems to be the only one grasping the full irony of the situation. Back outside again we luckily bump into The Don Earl blah blah fiftieth Duke of Monsville aka Charles Spencer. Apparently he regularly puts in personal walkabouts, although this is done with the subtle pretext that he's actually going about his day to day affairs. His manner is polite and brisk pausing occasionally, official papers or such under his arm, to talk to his subjects. The reaction is, somewhat like all things this 'big, bizarre'. You'd think Mickey Mouse had just put in an appearance as the crowds gather round to fawn, press flesh and gasp tenses. This is somewhat strange as Earl Spencer, previous to the death of his beloved sister, was ranked in the recognition stakes somewhere alongside one of the Queen's Corgies. Twin tugging frolicking pensioners are overheard to proclaim that their left hand's will remain unwashed for the foreseeable future after being graced with a handshake from the (supposedly) who-bleating childless wonder.

Next we head off up to the lake for our 'raison d'etre' and some proper Lady Diana, Queen of Hearts, cold and coffin action. And this, allegedly, is where it's at. We follow two middle-aged, and not surprisingly 'quite knowledgeable' members of the Red Cross who for no apparent reason are pushing a cripple-free wheelchair around a continuous circuit at breakneck speed about the Althorp estate. Diana as if you didn't know - currently resides in a tomb or

sleazenation

September/October 1998

Speak *(US)*

*'My walls are covered with bits of type
I want to use – they're like orphans
that you want to place in a good
home. Some stuff I'll have for years
before I'm able to find a use for it.'*

MARTIN VENEZKY

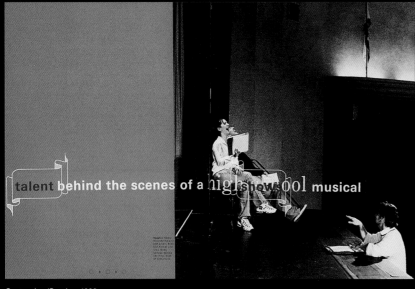

talent behind the scenes of a highschool musical

September/October 1998

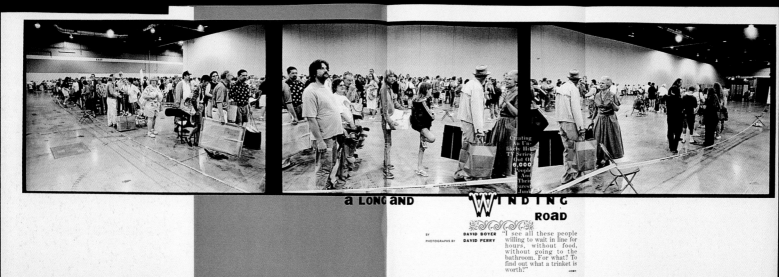

a LONG and WINDING ROAD

BY DAVID BOYER
PHOTOGRAPHS BY DAVID PERRY

"I see all these people willing to wait in line for hours, without food, without going to the bathroom. For what? To find out what a trinket is worth?"

Creating An Unlikely Hit TV Series Out Of 6,000 People And Their Dearest Junk

November/December 1998

BY THE TIME I GOT THROUGH THE FOREST, THE REVOLUTION WAS OVER AND THE PRESIDENT, HIS WIFE, AND HIS LIEUTENANT WERE SWINGING BY THEIR NECKS FROM THE LION-FACED GARGOYLES OF THE CATHEDRAL. The people stoned the corpses, which looked like gargoyles themselves, hardly human. I recalled seeing something like that in an old newsreel: Mussolini, dead and bloated, hanging upside down from the balcony of his apartment and wearing only a T-shirt and trousers, his people throwing stones. So much hate.

RON TANNER

September/October 1998

writer in a box

by Kevin Giordano

A writer's heart goes out to the classic authors for what Henry Miller called their "titanic efforts" to learn their craft. Steinbeck was cloistered in his father's garage for over 10 years honing his skills. Faulkner spun yarns from a roadhouse. Hemingway arm-wrestled with a journalism career while trying to pump out shorts on the side. Lawrence shacked up in a French countryside barn. Bukowski penned from the post office–the original "pedestrian gone postal." More recently, Toni Morrison, with two children in tow, wrote stories in the wee hours, and Harry Crews long-handed it on wood slabs until the sun came up.

College MFA programs are churning out writers in record numbers. But is anyone reading?

In the United States, however, the romantic vision of the writer hacking away in a shed has been shaken. The contemporary artist has been given an acceptable and promising alternative to flagellating himself in an attempt to write something publishable, and the late 20th century can now add something else to the list of things-made-easy in our society. Today's writer can conveniently circumvent his forefathers' struggle by enlisting in boot-camp for writers–the creative writing MFA program.

Musicians, dancers and visual artists have been fine-tuning their wares under the auspices of academia for centuries, yet the vision of the writer has never included a classroom. Writers are self-absorbed, gnarled, ugly and laid bare by their need to get it out. They don't sit in school learning terms like "authenticating detail" to describe what the greats did innately. Or do they?

November/December 1998

Speak was started in 1993 as a fashion and music magazine aimed at 18–29 year olds. Initially large format, it was strongly influenced by *Raygun*; David Carson designed its logo. But when financial and distribution pressures forced it to reduce its page size after issue six, art director Martin Venezky began to discover his own voice. The design became less frenetic and aggressive – the smaller page size meant that individual features ran over more pages, allowing the design to relax. At the same time the quality of content was improving so the legibility of material became more important. This change was announced on the front cover as the aggressively illegible original logo was

replaced by a more light-hearted, though equally unconventional, one.

The magazine sets itself against the mainstream, focusing on literature, art and personalities that are rarely covered in the commercial media. Venezky's design reflects this, avoiding current trends and instead following his own ideas. 'I'm always disappointed at how other magazines play safe. I just try to do things that interest and surprise me, and hope they also interest and surprise our readers. That way, I am never chasing after a current style or hipness.'

To achieve this he makes use of his collection of found type and imagery. 'Whenever I travel I visit flea markets and

antique stores. If something looks interesting – an old book or magazine, books of alphabets – I'll buy it and keep it until I find an opportunity to use it.' He saves old laser prints from other design jobs, filling notebooks with bits and pieces of type and image that can be re-used. 'I like imagery from earlier times but I try not to make fun of it or be ironic.' Scanning this material and combining it with modern typefaces on the computer enable Venezky to create his own world, one that has a very specific sensibility: 'A lot of current magazine design is very aggressive. Earlier fonts have a more human feel to them that helps overcome the dehumanizing nature of the computer.'

Summer 1999

January/February 1999

November/December 1999

Images

'We wanted to do something crude and basic. We spoke to a screen printer, showed him some Warhol stuff. He looked at it, said he could do it but added "Why don't you do it on your Mac?"'

LEE SWILLINGHAM, DAZED & CONFUSED

Magazines have always been a mix of word and image, the two elements combining in different ways to create the unique look and feel of each particular publication. Technology has played a major part in this relationship: the ability to reproduce word and image has consistently improved both in terms of quality and ease of production. Historically, the various advances in type technology – hotmetal, letraset, photosetting, etc. – created an emphasis on design with type; similarly advances such as halftone reproduction and four-colour litho forced the emphasis back to image.

More recently, the same technological influence can be seen at work with the computerization of magazine design. The possibilities raised by technology and type have been extensively explored since the advent of the Apple Mac, most prominently in the work of David Carson, but also in magazines generally. The magazine designer now has complete control of every typographic detail on every page of a magazine. It is only relatively recently, though, that magazine production has become so computer-orientated that imagery – photography and illustration – can benefit too. Here, the connection between technology and creativity has only just begun to be explored.

At its most basic, technology has made full-colour reproduction the norm; quality has improved while costs have reduced, leaving black-and-white reproduction as an option rather than the result of budget limitations. At the other end of the scale, the latest computer software can not only adjust colours and retouch blemishes, it can completely alter, combine and manipulate images. Such technology, alongside the increasing globalization of magazines, has served to push image to the forefront of current magazine design.

The catalyst for the renewed importance of image was *Colors* (Italy). *Colors* is paid for by the clothing firm Benetton and it brought together Italian photographer Oliviero Toscani and Hungarian-born graphic designer Tibor Kalman as Editorial Director and Editor-in-Chief respectively. Working alongside them on different issues were art directors such as Fernando Gutiérrez and Gary Koepke.

For a period in the mid-nineties *Colors* was the touchstone for any innovative new magazine launch. Its global nature – it described itself as 'a magazine about the rest of the world' and was published in a selection of dual-language editions – meant it relied on photography to put across ideas as clearly and boldly as possible. The cover of its launch issue (see page 36) was a typical example, featuring a just-born baby, complete with umbilical cord – a reference to the birth of a new magazine.

Colors developed a very distinctive visual style, combining small amounts of easily legible text with well-researched photography – a mixture of stock photography and commissioned work. The message that these pictures carried was crystal clear; sometimes, as in the AIDS issue, shockingly so.

It reached its zenith with Issue 13. This complete magazine was put together without words, using only photography to describe a loose narrative. As Kalman explained to Moira Cullen shortly after its publication (*Eye Magazine*, No 20, Vol 15), 'I wanted to see if we could create something visual that went beyond language. Issue 13 can be enjoyed in virtually the same way by a person in Vietnam as by a person in Uzbekistan or New York. I wanted to communicate this equality through pictures.' Fernando Gutiérrez, who was invited over to Rome by Kalman to art direct the issue, describes his involvement: 'It was a once in a lifetime experience. We had a great team of picture editors and great writers. It all started off with words – we had post-it notes of words for each spread – and it evolved from there.'

Colors foresaw how the globalization of culture, and in particular youth culture, meant there was an international audience for such projects. '*Colors* was about the end of nationality and the birth of subcultures', was how Kalman, who edited the first thirteen issues described the project. People from different countries were finding common links through fashion, music and art.

At the same time, new technology has made it simpler and cheaper to produce good quality independent magazines. While once projects such as *A Be Sea* (UK), and *Blow* (UK) were inhibited in what they could do by costs, now anyone with a computer can take some pictures, scan them and lay them out at home. The quality of such work may leave something to be desired, but the principle is there: the home publisher can produce material to a previously unheard of quality.

The high-end equipment used by professional repro houses has been revolutionized too – the relatively cheap cost of the new equipment leading to a reduction in the cost of their services. Thus many of the magazines featured in this book – *Big* (Spain, then later US), *SleazeNation* (UK) and *Self Service* (France) are three examples – have been able to launch and continue publishing to a global audience.

As well as generally opening up access to image reproduction, the new technology has begun to give the designer control over the actual process of reproduction; though how far this can go is unclear at present. Optimistic predictions that technology will hand complete control of image over to the computer-empowered designer in the same way that previous technology gave typographic control to the designer are unlikely to come true. As Christophe Gowans, art director of *Esquire* (UK), explains, 'Everybody wants to get to

Images

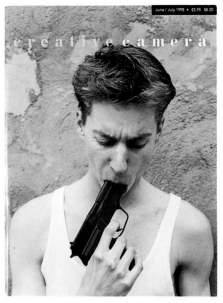

the future but the pre-digital age had got pretty slick; we're still getting unwanted surprises from digital imagery.' There remain too many unresolved issues to do with quality, proofing and consistency. 'These issues are turning designers into technicians, worrying about colour balances and file formats.'

What the technology can provide the designer with, though, is the ability to combine image and text on screen quickly and easily. Photoshop permits the designer to experiment with various effects in order to show the professionals at the repro house how they want the alteration or manipulation of the image to be carried out.

It is at these repro houses and photo labs, away from the design studio, that the possibilities offered by post-production of photography using high-end image manipulation systems such as Scitex and Paintbox are being explored.

Lee Swillingham and Stuart Spalding are perhaps a unique double-act, working together in art directing magazines. They first teamed up at *The Face* (UK), where in recognition of, and unwilling to compete with, the magazine's history of typographic innovation they deliberately focused on the imagery, in particular the fashion stories. They began to commission work from a new generation of photographers – people such as Norbert Schoerner and Inez Van Lamsweerde – who were beginning to apply digital manipulation to their pictures. '*The Face* pioneered the use of the Scitex as darkroom,' says Swillingham, 'That style is now taken for granted, there are books of it published now.'

Swillingham and Spalding are now art directing *Dazed & Confused* (UK), where all the pictures are post-produced to some extent. 'Even photographers known for their point-and-shoot aesthetic use it,' says Spalding, 'It's not an issue any more, it's normal.' While much of the photography is quietly and invisibly altered, other material is taking advantage of and experimenting with the computer systems to see what is possible. Some of this work is almost illustration.

Indeed, the line between photography and illustration is becoming increasingly blurred as one set of computer programs give the photographer new powers of manipulation while other programs give the illustrator the ability to build hyper-real renditions of people and objects.

However, like Gowans, Swillingham and Spalding acknowledge the problems digital imaging presents. They insist that the final images be presented for reproduction as either photographic prints or transparencies. 'We have no faith in electronic media,' admits Swillingham, 'It's a flaw in the process, but it's impossible to work without an actual original you can see. The photographers prefer this too.'

Illustrators generally don't face this problem. If their work is in electronic form it will have been originated on a computer rather than scanned in like a photograph; thus they, and the magazines that commission them, are happy for their work to be submitted either on a disc or via email.

Wallpaper (UK) can rightly claim to have single-handedly reintroduced illustration as a valid form of communication in magazines. Illustration had become the weaker of the visual contributions, as the ever-increasing obsession with celebrity and the increasing quality of the reproduction of photography led to photography's dominance. *Wallpaper* regard illustration as a vital and central part of the magazine, as designer Richard Seymour-Powell says, 'We treat illustration with respect, in the same way as any photography or writing we commission. We'll send an illustrator travelling to get a reference, and the fashion editor or interiors editor will style the illustration if necessary.'

This new interest in illustration has coincided with its computerization, as Christophe Gowans explains: 'Even people whose work doesn't look computer-generated are working on computer, using a pen and tablet to draw directly into the program.' He believes illustrators and photographers are learning from each other about the possibilities computers offer, and that the

whole process of image-creation has become far more collaborative as it becomes easier to keep on making alterations to a piece of work, be it illustration or photograph.

Whereas once it was clear when an illustration or photograph was finished – either the paint was dry or the photograph was developed – manipulation has made it easier to keep on changing, as Richard Seymour-Powell says, 'We're not scared of sending an item back three or four times until it's right.' With email and computers that can happen in one day.

Creative Camera *(UK, Issue 352, 1998) 210 x 280mm*
Designer *Phil Bicker*

Vanidad *(Spain, Issue 49, 1998) 230 x 300mm*
Art director *Fernando Gutiérrez*

The same image, by photographer Johannes Wohnseifer, appears on two magazine covers in very different contexts. *Creative Camera* uses it with no text except the magazine's name: the image is presented as art. *Vanidad*, however, uses the image as illustration, using its shock qualities as a metaphor for drug abuse.

In HIV+ people, it lives here.

Nei sieropositivi, il virus vive qui.

And here. E qui.

Our bodies are composed mostly of liquids. HIV lives in the body fluids of infected people. It lives in blood, semen, vaginal fluid, menstrual flow and breast milk. When body fluids pass from one person to another, the virus can get passed on too.

Il nostro corpo è costituito principalmente di liquidi. L'HIV vive nei liquidi biologici delle persone infette. Vive nel sangue, nello sperma, nelle secrezioni vaginali, nel flusso mestruale e nel latte materno. Nel momento in cui i liquidi biologici passano da un corpo a un altro, anche il virus può essere trasmesso.

BLOOD (left) in people who are infected has a high concentration of HIV. Even a very small amount of blood can transmit HIV. Any contact with infected blood can be dangerous.

IL SANGUE (a sinistra) delle persone infette ha un'alta concentrazione di virus HIV. Anche una piccolissima quantità di sangue infetto può trasmettere il virus. Qualsiasi contatto con sangue infetto può essere pericoloso.

SEMEN (above) not only has a very high concentration of HIV, it is usually transmitted in relatively large quantities. It is the most common carrier of HIV.

LO SPERMA (in alto) non solo ha un'altissima concentrazione di HIV, ma di solito viene trasmesso in quantità relativamente grandi. È il più comune mezzo di trasmissione dell'HIV.

18 COLORS

COLORS 19

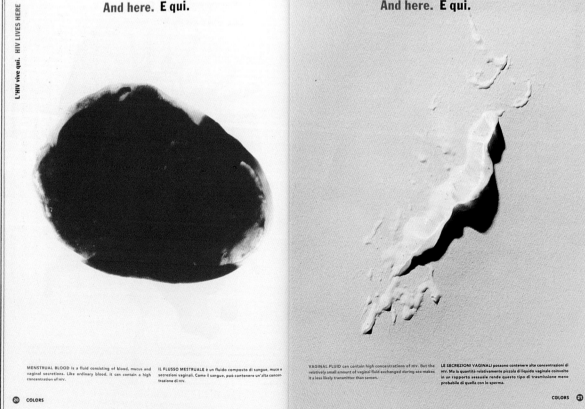

And here. E qui.

And here. E qui.

MENSTRUAL BLOOD is a fluid consisting of blood, mucus and vaginal secretions. Like ordinary blood, it can contain a high concentration of HIV.

IL FLUSSO MESTRUALE è un fluido composto di sangue, muco e secrezioni vaginali. Come il sangue, può contenere un'alta concentrazione di HIV.

VAGINAL FLUID can contain high concentrations of HIV. But the relatively small amount of vaginal fluid exchanged during sex makes it a less likely transmitter than semen.

LE SECREZIONI VAGINALI possono contenere alte concentrazioni di HIV. Ma la quantità relativamente piccola di liquido vaginale coinvolto in un rapporto sessuale rende questo tipo di trasmissione meno probabile di quella con lo sperma.

20 COLORS

COLORS 21

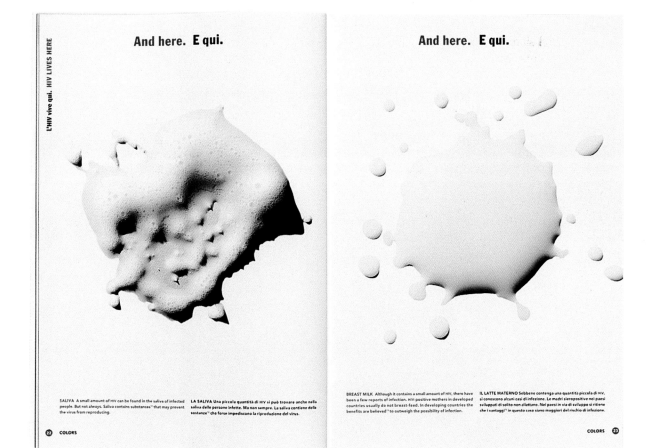

And here. E qui.

And here. E qui.

And here. E qui.

L'HIV vive qui. HIV LIVES HERE

SALIVA A small amount of HIV can be found in the saliva of infected people. But not always. Saliva contains substances[1] that may prevent the virus from reproducing.

LA SALIVA Una piccola quantità di HIV si può trovare anche nella saliva delle persone infette. Ma non sempre. La saliva contiene delle sostanze[1] che forse impediscono la riproduzione del virus.

BREAST MILK Although it contains a small amount of HIV, there have been a few reports of infection. HIV-positive mothers in developed countries usually do not breast-feed. In developing countries the benefits are believed[1] to outweigh the possibility of infection.

IL LATTE MATERNO Sebbene contenga una quantità piccola di HIV, si conoscono alcuni casi di infezione. Le madri sieropositive nei paesi sviluppati di solito non allattano. Nei paesi in via di sviluppo si ritiene che i vantaggi[1] in questo caso siano maggiori del rischio di infezione.

22 COLORS

COLORS 23

Colors (Italy, Issue 7, 1994) 190 x 270mm
Subtitled 'A magazine about the rest of the world', *Colors* foresaw the importance of globalization. Every issue is published in six different dual-language versions, each one pairing English with either Croatian, French, German, Italian Russian or Spanish, emphasizing its global nature.
Working alongside these combinations of languages, the photography has a unique importance in expressing ideas and concepts. These spreads from an issue about AIDS are typical: showing fluids in which the HIV virus lives, the photographs are shocking in their simplicity and frankness.
Art director *Scott Stowell*
Editor-in-chief *Tibor Kalman*

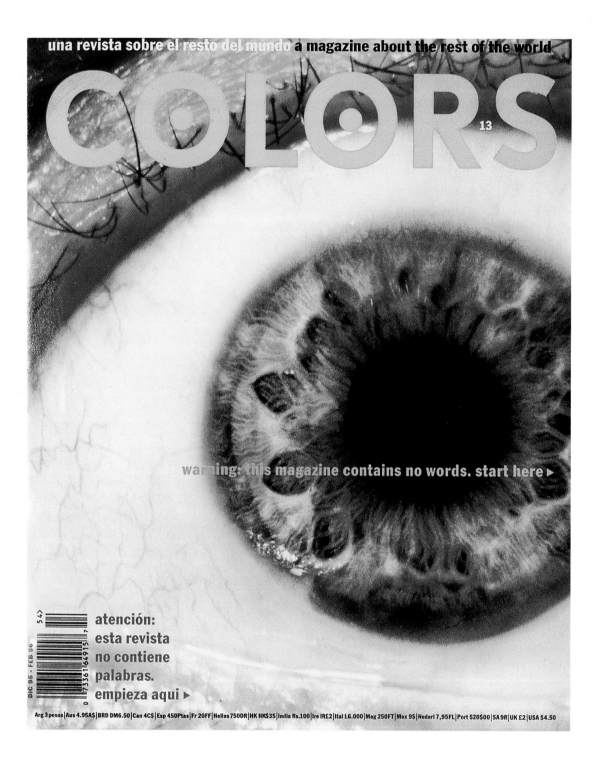

una revista sobre el resto del mundo **a magazine about the rest of the world**

COLORS 13

warning: this magazine contains no words. start here ▶

atención:
esta revista
no contiene
palabras.
empieza aqui ▶

Arg 3 pesos|Aus 4.95A$|BRD DM6.50|Can 4C$|Esp 450Ptas|Fr 20FF|Hellas 750DR|HK HK$35|India Rs.100|Ire IR£2|Ital L6.000|Mag 250FT|Mex 9$|Nederl 7,95FL|Port 520$00|SA 9R|UK £2|USA $4.50

Colors (Italy, Issue 13, 1995) 230 x 287mm
'Warning: this magazine contains no words…', states the cover, taking the desire to achieve a global language to its extreme. There follow 88 pages of painstakingly researched pictures. Working with a team of picture researchers and writers (each page started as a series of keywords) the design and editorial team worked out a loose narrative that lets the reader bring their own meanings to the pages while still maintaining a visual pace. It includes a spread, pp68/9, featuring a mock headline, standfirst and picture captions.
Art director *Fernando Gutiérrez*
Editor-in-Chief *Tibor Kalman*
Picture research *Paola Cimmino, Alfredo Albertone and Manuela Fugenzi*

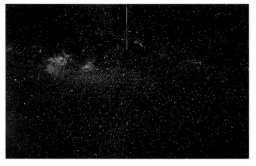

pp 2, 3

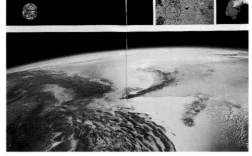

pp 4, 5

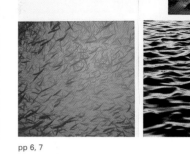

pp 6, 7

pp 8, 9

pp 10, 11

pp 12, 13

pp 14, 15

pp 16, 17

pp 18, 19

pp 20, 21

pp 22, 23

pp 24, 25

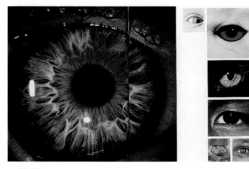

pp 26, 27

pp 28, 29

pp 32, 33

pp 34, 35

pp 36, 37

pp 38, 39

pp 40, 41

pp 42, 43

pp 44, 45

pp 46, 47

pp 48, 49

pp 50, 51

pp 52, 53

pp 54, 55

pp 56, 57

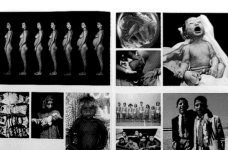

pp 58, 59

pp 60, 61

pp 62, 63

pp 64, 65

pp 66, 67

pp 68, 69

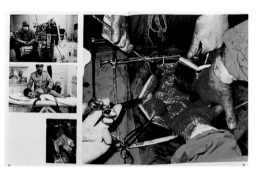

pp 70, 71

pp 72, 73

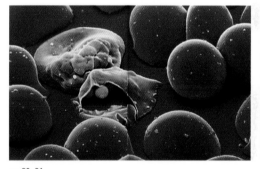

pp 74, 75

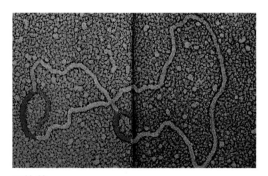

pp 76, 77

pp 78, 79

pp 80, 81

pp 82, 83

pp 84, 85

pp 86, 87

Issue 1, Summer 1997

Issue 2, Autumn 1998

Issue 3, Winter 1998/9

Nest *(US) 230 x 280mm*
Architectural details and fabric patterns are used as frames for photographic examinations of modern interiors, giving this relatively new magazine a feeling of longevity and authority.
Art director *Joseph Holtzman*

Vogue Hommes International Mode *(Italy, Issue 6, Autumn 1999/Winter 2000) 225 x 297mm*

All the photography in this issue played with the idea of lack of control. For these examples, professional photographers were briefed and sent to various parts of the world to art direct shots by local itinerant photographers. Other stories in the issue include work by photographers unknown to the art director, and a shoot where all the models' faces have been swapped.

Art director Phil Bicker

There are models who are flavour of the moment and then there are models like Gisele Bündchen.
She has charisma and charm. She has a body that women would genuinely kill for and she is addicted to sweets.
She comes from Brazil, but we're prepared to follow her just about anywhere...

SPOT

Photograph Terry Richardson

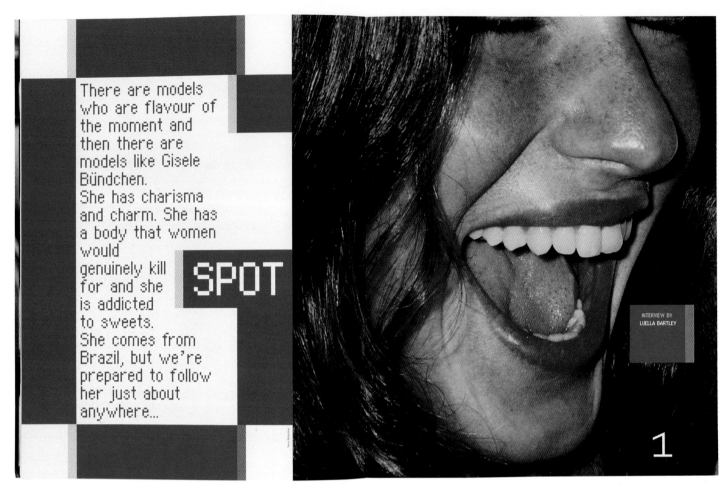

INTERVIEW BY
LUELLA BARTLEY

1

Big *(US, Issue 23, Summer 1999) 240 x 305mm*
A unique project featuring photographs of one girl – Brazilian model Giselle – by 21 leading fashion photographers. Each photographer had to pitch their idea to the art directors who then planned the shoots to happen across a two week period, later editing and pacing the resulting pictures to create an extraordinarily varied collection of images of one person. Technology played a major part in the project – most of the images have been retouched or manipulated to some extent, while the latest 3D modelling programs were used to create the computer renditions of Giselle (OPPOSITE, TOP RIGHT).
Art directors *Lee Swillingham & Stuart Spalding*

Photographs Paul Weatherall

Image Solve Sundsbo & Alex Rutherford, Digital manipulation Lost In Space

Photographs Chris Moore

Photograph Vincent Peters

Photograph Lee Jenkins

Photographs Elaine Constantine

Photograph Elaine Constantine

Photographs Terry Richardson

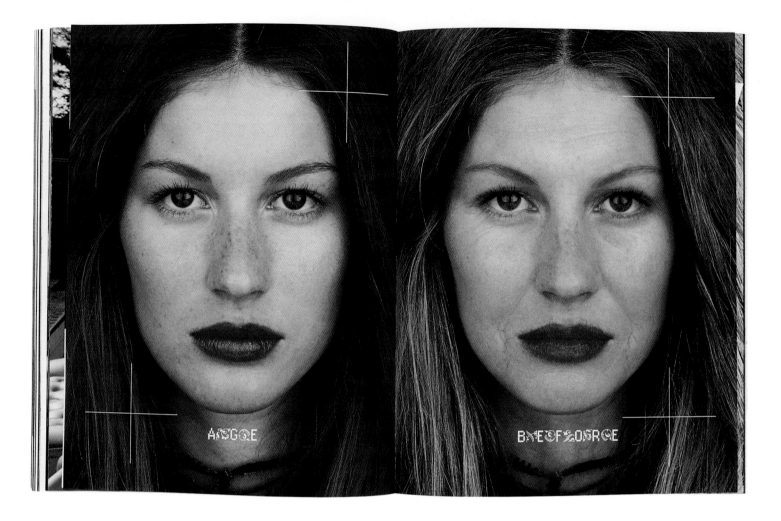

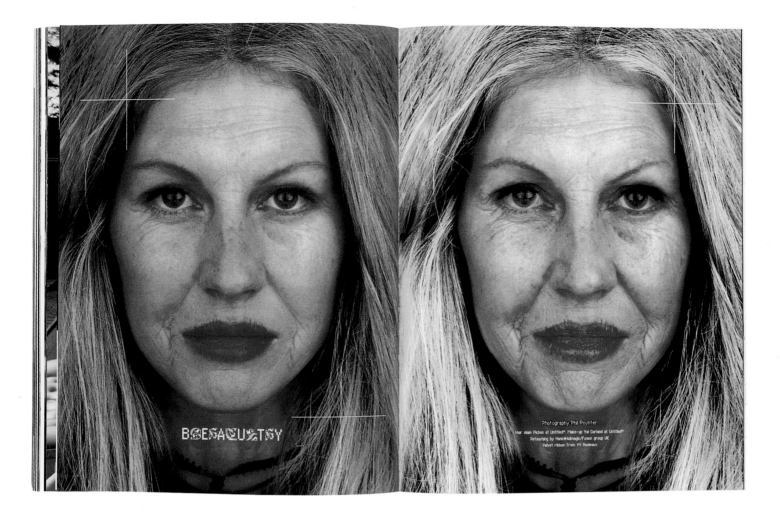

BEAUTY

Photography Phil Poynter
Hair Alain Pichon at Untitled®. Make-up Val Garland at Untitled®.
Retouching by Hank@Admagic/Fusion group UK
Velvet ribbon from YV Rouleaux

Big *(US, Issue 23, Summer 1999) 240 x 305mm*
The power of digital image manipulation: these four images
show convincingly how Giselle might look as she ages.
Art directors *Lee Swillingham & Stuart Spalding*
Photographs *Phil Poynter*
Retouching *Hank at Admagic/Fusion Group UK*

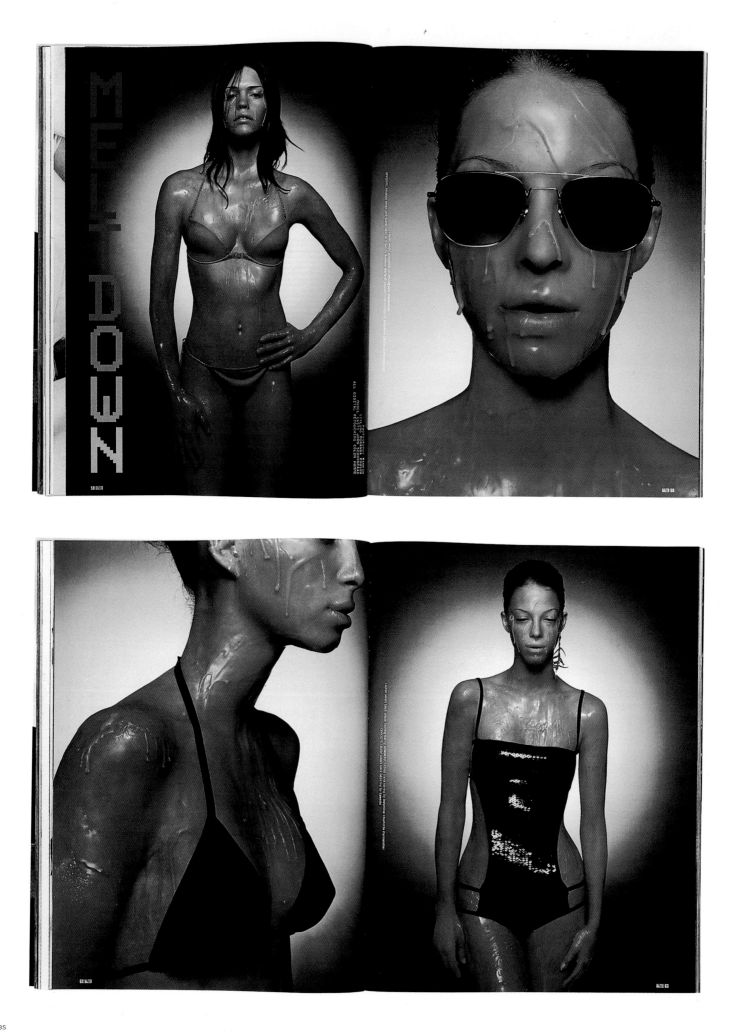

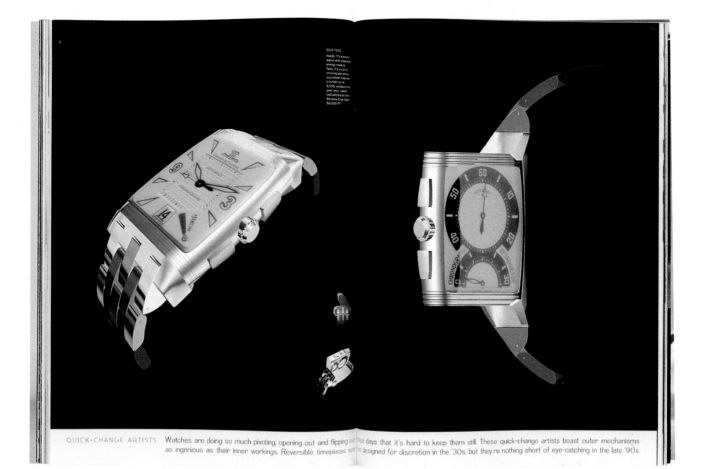

COIN TOSS
Heads, it's a basic watch with a back-up energy reserve. Tails, it's a sporty chronograph with a countdown feature. Limited run of 5,000, available this year only. Jaeger LeCoultre's all-new Reverso Gran Sport, 59,000 FF.

QUICK-CHANGE ARTISTS   Watches are doing so much pivoting, opening out and flipping these days that it's hard to keep them still. These quick-change artists boast outer mechanisms as ingenious as their inner workings. Reversible timepieces were not designed for discretion in the '30s, but they're nothing short of eye-catching in the late '90s

OPPOSITE   **Dazed & Confused** *(UK, Issue 57, August 1999) 230 x 300mm*
Art directors *Lee Swillingham & Stuart Spalding*
Photographer *Rankin*

THIS PAGE   **Vogue Hommes International Mode**
(Italy, Issue 6, Autumn 1999/Winter 2000) 228 x 297mm
Art director *Phil Bicker*
Illustrator *Ora-Ito*

Examples from two fashion stories that show how photography and illustration are merging with each other. The *Dazed & Confused* photographs have been so heavily and convincingly post-produced that they could be hyper-real illustration; meanwhile *Vogue Hommes* has used computer illustration rather than still-life photography to show the latest watches.

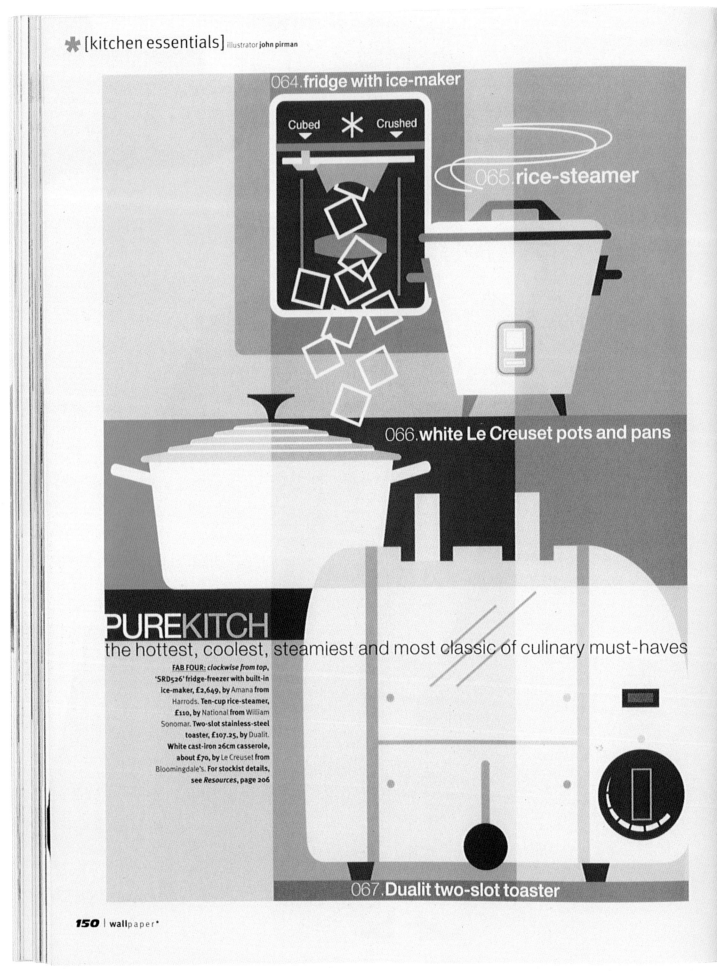

064.**fridge with ice-maker**

Cubed ✳ Crushed

065.rice-steamer

066.**white Le Creuset pots and pans**

PUREKITCH
the hottest, coolest, steamiest and most classic of culinary must-haves

FAB FOUR: *clockwise from top,*
**'SRD526' fridge-freezer with built-in
ice-maker, £2,649, by** Amana from
Harrods. **Ten-cup rice-steamer,
£110, by** National from William
Sonomar. **Two-slot stainless-steel
toaster, £107.25, by** Dualit.
**White cast-iron 26cm casserole,
about £70, by** Le Creuset from
Bloomingdale's. **For stockist details,
see** *Resources,* **page 206**

067.**Dualit two-slot toaster**

Issue 8, January/February 1998. Illustrator John Pirman

Issue 5, July/August 1997. Illustrator Michael Economy

Issue 13, September/October 1998. Illustrator Lotta Kühlhorn

Issue 5, July/August 1997. Illustration Softroom

Wallpaper *(UK) 230 x 300mm*
Aiming at an ultra-fashionable international reader, this interiors magazine takes its visual appearance very seriously. By championing illustration it has been almost single-handedly responsible for its reintroduction as a valid form of magazine imagery. These examples show how it is used throughout the magazine: to show products (OPPOSITE); as icons to break up news pages (THIS PAGE, TOP); to open features (THIS PAGE, CENTRE); and to demonstrate ideas (BOTTOM).
Art director *Herbert Winkler*

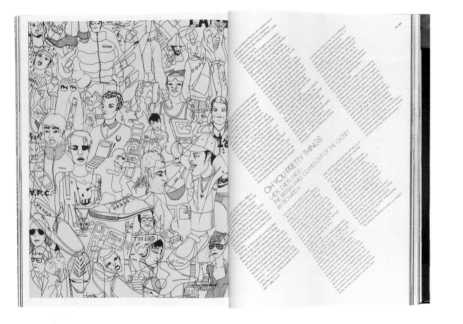

TOP **Esquire** *(UK, September 1999) 215 x 290mm*
Art director *Christophe Gowans*
Illustrator *Christopher Kasch*

CENTRE **Arena Homme Plus** *(UK, Issue 12, Autumn 1999/Winter 2000) 230 x 300mm*
Art director *Stephen Baillie*
Illustrator *Giles Deacon*

BOTTOM **Flaunt** *(US, Issue 5, June/July 1999) 228 x 275mm*
Art directors *Eric Roinestad & Jim Turner*
Illustrator *Malcolm Hill*

Illustration becomes hip once more; after a period where its use has been limited to providing pictorial decoration to pieces of fiction, illustration is everywhere again as these spreads show: depicting the piece's subject, comedian Sean Hughes, in the situation he is writing about (ESQUIRE); introducing an opinion piece about the British male (ARENA HOMME PLUS); and finally, still helping to attract the reader to a piece of fiction (FLAUNT).

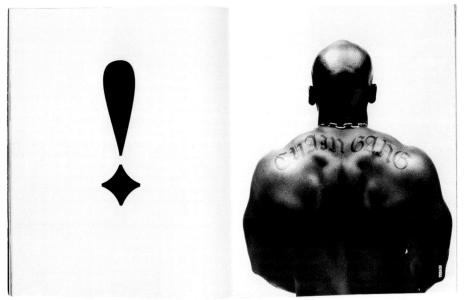

Blag *(UK, Issues 1, 2, 4, 1992–1996) 215 x 280mm*
As with the covers of this independent magazine (SEE PAGE 61),
the content is uncompromising. A loose mix of mainly image
and some text, it is held together by its single-minded attitude
and by the careful design and pacing of its pages.
Design Yacht Associates

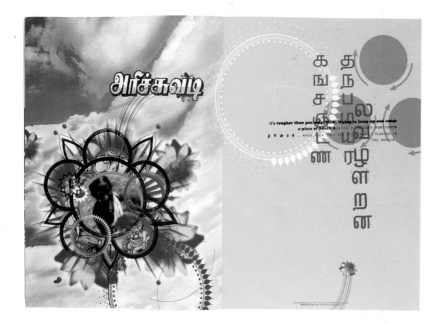

i-Jusi (*South Africa, Issue 6, 1997*) *237 x 420mm*
This bi-annual magazine is published by Orange Juice Design to encourage and promote South African graphic design worldwide. Designers, design students, illustrators, photographers and writers are encouraged to explore their personal views on life in the new South Africa. Art director *Garth Walker*

Issue 1, 1998

Econy *(Germany)*

'We had to find the photographers who would bring the right aesthetic to the magazine – not the normal business magazine photography where the lens is pointing up at the great businessman.'

MIKE MEIRÉ

Issue 2, 1998

Issue 2, 1998

Issue 4, 1999

AUFHÖREN? ACH WAS.

UNTERNEHMERGEIST MUSS MIT DEM ALTER NICHT SCHWINDEN.
DER BEWEIS? WERNER OTTO, 88 JAHRE.

Issue 2, 1998

Econy (it's a made-up word, but refers to economy) was set up in response to the standard, stuffy business magazines. These magazines ignored the new generation of business people, the new entrepreneurs that have set up businesses in fashion, music and media over the past five years. These people were different, unlike the previous generation of business people, so *Econy* was to be different too.

Art director Mike Meiré was clear that to merely have more relevant content was not enough. Such a new idea had to look new and be relevant to its media-aware target audience. '*Econy* came along at exactly the right time,'

he explains, 'I had this idea for a very constructed layout. David Carson's ideas, which I loved initially, had become very tired.' So he designed the exact opposite – a very tight set of limitations, playing off black-and-white typography (Univers and Times) against colour photography. Meiré calls it a liquid identity – a very strong identity that has an inbuilt provision for change and development. 'Sometimes now there are too many options. Limitations are good.'

The photographic element was key to making the magazine different to other business titles. 'I spent six months looking at photographers' books. I wanted to use the

type of photography our audience know from music and fashion magazines to ensure they related to the new project.' The resulting portraits feature business people as real people, in their busy studios and offices where people are rushing about, where there is lots of activity.

Still life photography is used too, a difference being established by avoiding the hackneyed lighting tricks so often used to try and make objects look 'cool'. Instead all such material is shot as naturally as possible, with a knowing nod toward fashion where possible, such as the use of the 'right' fabric behind an object.

IT'S BEEN A LANG, LANG TIME

HELMUT LANG GILT ALS DER EINFLUSSREICHSTE MODE-DESIGNER DER NEUNZIGER JAHRE.
DURCH SEINEN UMZUG NACH NEW YORK HAT ER SICH DEN MARKT DER ZUKUNFT ERSCHLOSSEN.
AN SEINER VISION MUSS DAS NICHTS ÄNDERN.

Issue 4, 1999

KOPF ODER ZAHL?

ZWEI DOKTORANDEN GRÜNDEN GEMEINSAM EINE FIRMA.
EINER BEISST SICH DURCH – UND WIRD ZUM VORZEIGE-UNTERNEHMER.
DER ANDERE WIRD LIEBER PROFESSOR ALS REICH.

01 GUNNAR BRINK, BIOTUL-CHEF. 02 ULRICH HOFMANN, BIOPHYSIKER.

Issue 4, 1999

HOME-RUN

TELEWORKING WIRD ZUR NORMALEN ARBEITSFORM DER INFORMATIONSGESELLSCHAFT.
NOCH ABER RINGT DIE ARBEIT VON ZU HAUSE AUS MIT VORURTEILEN UND DOGMEN.

01 ZU HAUSE ARBEITEN ...
02 ... ODER IM BÜRO?

Issue 4, 1999

Credits / Index

Thank you to:

All the art directors, designers, editors and publishers whose help, advice and co-operation made this book possible.

Richard Dean, who photographed all the magazines and the images for the chapter heading pages.

Jo, Paul, Felicity and Laurence at Laurence King.

Lewis Blackwell.

Lorenzo Beraldo, Phil Bicker, Neville Brody, John Brown, Patrick Burgoyne, Veronica Burke, Ian Chilvers, Stephen Coates, Paul Davies, Robin Derrick, Petra Dworschak, Tony Elliott, Simon Esterson, Detlef Fiedler, Vince Frost, Mercia Fuoco, Etienne Gilfallin, Caroline Guest, Fernando Gutiérrez, Peter Hall, Paul Harpin, Andreas Hoyer, Alexander Isley, Conny Kahl, Verena Kohler, Mike Lackersteen, Vic Lime, Rami Lipa, Domenic Lippa, Paul Makovsky, Yolande Muelas, Carlos Mustienes, Quentin Newark, Robert Newman, Lionel Openshaw, Mark Ponder at HeronPrint, Matthew Preston, Will Scott, William Seighart, James Spagnoletti, Holger Struck, Jake Tilson, Stephen Todd, Teal Triggs, Franca Tubiana, Bonnie Vaughan.

Cover photographs by Jeremy Leslie

Dedicated to Lesley

Further reading:

W. Owen, *Magazine Design* (1991), Laurence King, ISBN 1 85669 003 2

Credits / Index